There's No Traffic
on the Extra Mile

There's No Traffic on the Extra Mile

Lessons on the Road from Dreams to Destiny

RICKEY MINOR

GOTHAM
BOOKS

GOTHAM BOOKS
Published by Penguin Group (USA) Inc.
375 Hudson Street, New York, New York 10014, U.S.A.
Penguin Group (Canada), 90 Eglinton Avenue East, Suite 700, Toronto, Ontario
M4P 2Y3, Canada (a division of Pearson Penguin Canada Inc.); Penguin Books
Ltd, 80 Strand, London WC2R 0RL, England; Penguin Ireland, 25 St Stephen's
Green, Dublin 2, Ireland (a division of Penguin Books Ltd); Penguin Group
(Australia), 250 Camberwell Road, Camberwell, Victoria 3124, Australia (a divi-
sion of Pearson Australia Group Pty Ltd); Penguin Books India Pvt Ltd, 11
Community Centre, Panchsheel Park, New Delhi—110 017, India; Penguin
Group (NZ), 67 Apollo Drive, Rosedale, North Shore 0632, New Zealand (a divi-
sion of Pearson New Zealand Ltd); Penguin Books (South Africa) (Pty) Ltd, 24
Sturdee Avenue, Rosebank, Johannesburg 2196, South Africa

Penguin Books Ltd, Registered Offices: 80 Strand, London WC2R 0RL, England

Published by Gotham Books, a member of Penguin Group (USA) Inc.

First printing, January 2009
10 9 8 7 6 5 4 3 2 1

LIBRARY OF CONGRESS CATALOGING-IN-PUBLICATION DATA

Minor, Rickey.
    There's no traffic on the extra mile : lessons on the road from dreams to
destiny / by Rickey Minor.
        p. cm.
    ISBN 978-1-592-40418-6 (hardcover)
    1. Success. 2. Minor, Rickey. I. Title.
BJ1611.2.M515 2009
650.1—dc22   2008042234

Printed in the United States of America
Set in New Aster LT Std. • Designed by Sabrina Bowers

While the author has made every effort to provide accurate telephone numbers
and Internet addresses at the time of publication, neither the publisher nor the
author assumes any responsibility for errors, or for changes that occur after
publication. Further, the publisher does not have any control over and does not
assume any responsibility for author or third-party Web sites or their content.

Dedicated to my wife, Karen, and son, Sean

We all have dreams. But in order to make dreams into reality, it takes an awful lot of determination, dedication, self-discipline, and effort.
—JESSE OWENS

Contents

Foreword

By QUINCY JONES

Welcome to *The Extra Mile*, where true champions break away from the pack. The first time I met Rickey Minor, I recognized that along with his extraordinary musical talent, he has a winning personality and an undying dedication to creative excellence. The networks and the stars come to Rickey for good reason: He knows just how to push someone with already proven talent to the next level in a manner that's simultaneously supportive and unfiltered.

From the first time that I saw him in action, something about Rickey reminded me a little bit of myself. He was working as music director for Whitney Houston and playing bass at a rehearsal for the Billboard Music Awards. I walked into the room and the band was kickin'. I mean the strings were soaring, the horns were poppin', the singers were wailin', and the rhythm was groovin'. Right in the middle of it all was Rickey, thumpin' that bass. Then Whitney made her entrance and blew the roof off that place.

After the rehearsal I took Rickey aside and told him that I had always wanted to work with Whitney. She's amazing. Our conversation went on and we talked about playing, arranging, and conducting. Although we come from different places and different times, we share a considerable amount of common ground. We both come from very humble roots, and frankly neither of us was exactly an obvious candidate to take the world stage, much less to conduct once we got there.

To be certain, Rickey has his own unique talents and musical gifts, but something about his work ethic and wide range of musical interests felt very familiar to me. At one time or another, anybody who ever picks up the baton has to think about the next generation. Make no mistake, I'm still very much in the race, but it's always good to know that there's someone like Rickey who's ready to pick up that baton and really run with it. He looks at each challenge that he faces and embraces it wholeheartedly, pushing the boundaries and elevating each project with a steady hand.

I remember once watching Rickey conduct for my lifelong friend Ray Charles. Afterward, the two of us spoke for a while about that incredible feeling of standing onstage with a big band in front of us, waiting for the downbeat.

In music, the downbeat means it's time to get down to some serious business. The cats that can really play live for the chance to be in the moment and really start cooking. In the rhythm of our lives, the downbeat is just as momentous. In fact, some of us spend our whole lives just waiting for that special downbeat. In this book Rickey shows you how to listen for that big downbeat in your own life, signaling that the time has finally come for you to start moving toward your goals.

Knowledge really can be power and passing on whatever knowledge and wisdom we gain is both a responsibility and a joy. One of many things that impresses me about Rickey is the way that he takes the time to bring so many young people into his working environment whenever possible. As the saying goes, "If you can see it, you can be it," and I just know that one of those kids watching Rickey is going to step up soon and make us both very proud.

Rickey believes that each and every one of us is a "work

in progress," whether we're just starting off or at the top of our game. His stories show us how some of the most powerful lessons come at times and in situations when we least expect them. His words remind me of the many nights I spent learning directly from the legends in clubs and concert halls around the world. Those are the lessons that really matter—the ones where we learn by example.

Many of us in the music business admire and respect Rickey, and his success story has been a truly beautiful thing to watch unfold. In *There's No Traffic on the Extra Mile*, he's found the perfect vehicle to pass along so many of the invaluable lessons he had to learn along the way, often the hard way. That means this book is not simply about Rickey's heartening success story—it can be about yours too.

To succeed in this world doing what you love is the ultimate dream, but it's a dream you have to work extremely hard to make come true. Herbie Hancock, one of the musical giants of our time, once put it beautifully: "Out of our beliefs are born deeds; out of our deeds we form habits; out of our habits grows our character; and on our character we build our destiny."

Rickey demonstrates true character onstage and off. As you are about to see, he stands as a shining example of how to put your heart and soul into everything you do. In the end, in life as in music, it all comes down to heart and soul. My buddy Ray Charles once said, "What is soul? It's like electricity—we don't really know what it is, but it's a force that can light a room." Rickey Minor has been lighting up rooms wherever he goes, and he's done it by going the extra mile. That's how Rickey turned his dreams into his destiny, and that's how you can too.

One of my favorite sayings goes, "The heart of art is in the living and the heart of living is in the loving."

There may be no traffic on the extra mile, as Rickey likes to say, but thanks to his inspiring and motivational words in this book, those who get there will soon find themselves in excellent company.

The day I met Quincy.
WOW!

Introduction

Regardless of where we start, whether it's rags or riches, we all face the same types of challenges in trying to create lives of purpose, fulfillment, and adventure for ourselves. Toward that end, there are plenty of inspirational teachers and mentors out there who are eager to share their wisdom with you, lift your spirits, and fill you with hope. These experts have produced thousands of self-help books, but unfortunately, one of their most common complaints is the sense that so few who buy their books actually do anything constructive with the information they offer.

In contrast to some of the other books on the shelf, what I give you on these pages has a slightly different perspective. I've seen a lot over the past three decades on the front lines of this dream factory called the entertainment business. Behind each story are little clues to the puzzle called success, some very serious and others more lighthearted. But every one of the elements I describe has the power to thrust you forward in the pursuit of your dreams—or stop you dead in your tracks.

Sadly, too many inspirational and self-help books don't fulfill their purpose because the reader is seldom ready to make the necessary changes to their habits and behaviors. You've heard it all over and over again: Get off the sofa and exercise more. Ease up on the beer and junk food. Quit the donuts. Stop smoking. Turn off the TV. Read a book! Yeah, right. And we wonder why today's generation of young adults will be the first in the last century, according to an article in *The Wall Street Journal,* who will not live as long or be as wealthy as their parents.

The stories I have to share will show the enormous potential and amazing talent in each and every one of us—and they will point out all the trap doors we often fall into, the intricate and sometimes extremely silly things we do that completely mess things up.

My ultimate goal is to give you a peek through the curtains. Whether you are a big fan of *American Idol* or a popular music lover, or someone with minimal interest in either, I hope these stories will make you stop and notice things that you may have ignored or discounted as inconsequential before.

You'll see on these pages that there are a great many reasons why 99 percent of us fail at realizing our dreams, or even our "Plan B." There are also myriad factors that have to come together to make things happen for that 1 percent who succeed. The great news is that most of these elements are within your control. Even better is that you don't need to be a brain surgeon to understand them.

If I could give a single formula behind any success I've experienced, from early childhood to this present moment, including the act of writing this book, it would be:

Always give people more than they expect.

That sounds pretty simple, doesn't it? True, it is a simple thought. Most would agree that it seems like good common sense. What I trust you will realize quickly in the next few pages and chapters is how fascinating and tricky it can be to put this formula into action. You may find that by following this principle you will beat out people with more natural talent than you have. You'll start to get noticed—and find yourself on the radar. You'll also have to stay alert in case any of your enemies from within—your own ego and its good friends, arrogance, greed, and complacency—begin to rear their ugly heads.

Let me be honest with you. As music director on *American Idol*, half of what I do is the art, the skill, and the time I put in. I can freely say that there are thousands of people who are capable of doing what I do: providing the arrangements, finding the perfect musicians, and conducting the orchestra. The other 50 percent is something that you're either born with or that you're able to develop. It's the ability to work with people.

As you will read, music is the path that has taken me places, introduced me to people, and put me in situations that, in retrospect, seem to have unfolded in a natural progression toward my goals—although the route has been winding and challenging at times.

But whether your dream is to be a singer, a fashion designer, a carpenter, or an architect, you have to drive toward your passion. Sometimes, identifying and developing this passion involves some trial and error, but it also takes a plan. You need to outline the steps that it will take to move forward in your life, and you have to be truthful with yourself about the obstacles to success. If you can see these obstacles coming and jump out of their way, you will save time and energy for the next level of challenges that lie ahead.

The thing that will make the critical difference is your drive to go that extra mile. When you put this into practice, you'll separate yourself very quickly from the pack—not tomorrow or next week, but today. As you leave everyone else behind, you'll wonder why so few are willing to put in that extra effort. Can't they see it too? There's no traffic on the extra mile.

There's No Traffic
on the Extra Mile

PART ONE

Getting Started

GO WEST!

I grew up in South Central Los Angeles, Watts to be specific. It is a place where a lot of people end up staying for the rest of their lives, whether they prefer it that way or have no other choice.

There are many places throughout the world that look, smell, and feel exactly like South Central. These types of places are usually reserved for people who are all but invisible to the rest of society. These are the neighborhoods situated on the outskirts of the city proper where you come to stay as a last option—when you can't afford to live anywhere else. In New York, Chicago, Detroit, Washington, D.C., London, Paris, or Rio, you'll see the same kind of slums, where the air is thick with despair and hopelessness. Despite it all, there's an enduring culture of love, family, and community that has a vibrant pulse. People go to church and talk on their porches or in their front yards. Children play, skip rope, and frolic in the water of the fire hydrant in the summer.

Like every other kid in Watts, I didn't know that there was any other way of living. I got up. I rode my bike, got chased by dogs, laughed with my friends, and ate Popsicles. I didn't question things. I did the best I knew how to go through life happily. But as I got a little bit older, I began to feel a drive inside myself. I knew innately there was more for me waiting outside the neighborhood. It's hard to say whether I was born that way or if it was something I learned, or a combination of both.

For me, it has never been about getting away from Watts and the people of my community, about being richer, or about achieving something bigger and better than where I came from. For as long as I can remember, those things have not driven my ambition. It's all been about achieving my *personal best*.

I was actually born and spent the first eight years of my life in Monroe, Louisiana. It was a small town, mostly dirt roads, and the few that were paved didn't have any sidewalks. The most exciting thing in town was Saturday night at the Elks Club: the B.Y.O.B. (bring your own bottle) dance with a disc jockey playing records. This was the early to mid 1960s, and the Klan was all around, too. Living in such a tense, segregated place made a deep impression on me. Even as a small child, it bothered me that people of different races weren't working together. I'm certain that those early memories have driven me to make sure that I work with all races, ethnicities, and genders.

My grandmother Donia Minor was the matriarch of our family. She moved to Los Angeles with my aunt Dixie after going out there to visit her sister Anna in 1967, and she never returned to Louisiana. She had the incredible vision to say, "We all need to be in California. This is the place where we need to be." Hers was that kind of matriarchal energy that never allowed dust to settle, and she knew exactly what needed to be done right on the spot. She took care of business, and made sure that I, her grandson, did my share as well. She always dressed like she was going somewhere, with the hemline of her skirts cut just below the knee. She wore a tightly cropped wig and glasses that were the fashion of the time. I don't think she owned a pair of tennis shoes.

From an early age, I was aware that my grandmother had risked everything when she moved to California without a concrete plan or any guarantees. She worked as a house-keeper for the actor Steve McQueen, taking the bus to his beach house in Malibu. She saved enough money to get a one-bedroom apartment of her own that was always spick-and-span. It wasn't long before she got a larger space and sent for my uncle Frank and my stepfather John Blevins. Soon after that, the rest of the family came out on the bus. It took three days to go across country in the sweltering heat of the summer. I was eight years old.

Since I was the eldest boy, I lived with my grandmother and my uncle Daniel (who is hearing impaired) during the school week. On weekends, I stayed with my mother, stepfather and my four siblings, Kathyrn, Victor, Cheryl, and John, Jr. We lived in the Jordan Downs Housing Projects in Watts, three bedrooms and one bathroom.

After going back to school, my mother, Helen Blevins, became a nurse—she worked the three P.M. to eleven P.M. shift at St. Francis Hospital in Lynwood, California. My stepfather, John Blevins, got a job as a carpet layer for a company that operated out of Hollywood. Things were starting to look up.

I was awed by the courage my grandmother had to stop, pick up everything, and move to another location to pursue a better way of life. Go west. The thought of what she did challenged me and continues to inspire me today. I thought, "If she can do that from there, then I can go anywhere."

I always knew I was not going to be defined or limited by my circumstances. I learned that happiness was not based on having what you want but wanting what you have. It is as simple as saying to oneself, "This is my room. It's not very big, but it is so much better than what I started with."

When life serves you what you believe is unjust and unfair, always remember, your roots are your strength and your foundation. They are not your limitations, and should never become your excuse.

THE PURPLE CHEVY

Whenever my uncle Frank had to get gas or wash his purple Chevrolet Impala, he'd always invite me to ride along. On these trips and others, he showed me the city. It was a big thing to get out of the neighborhood, to see the palm trees in Hollywood and everything else between the ocean and the mountains of L.A.

This exposure to life outside the projects must have made a difference. Not that I was that much more worldly than the others in my community. The universe I perceived was measured in just tens of miles. I was years away from taking my first airplane ride. It was hard looking at a map and imagining other cultures and languages beyond my own. People from foreign countries talked funny, and I had little consideration that they might think the same of me.

Perhaps it comes as no big surprise that the title of this book stems from that metaphor of driving a car. The trips in that purple Impala represented the discovery of a universe of limitless possibilities in my young mind. Remarkably, that feeling has never left me.

Today, the destinations on my daily drive, as I replay it in my mind, may be all about fulfilling commitments and responsibilities, my accelerator keeping up the pace to stay on schedule. But in some ways, I remain as impressionable as the young Rickey, with a sense of wonder and gratitude at the mystery of how things unfold.

I always looked up to Uncle Frank. He was truly a father figure to me, since I never met my own. He was six feet tall and thin, he dressed well, and he embodied that deep sense of social consciousness of the 1960s. But suddenly, he was gone. He was drafted to Vietnam, where he would spend the next three years. In the void of his absence, I could have fallen through the cracks, but he had taught me something valuable that stuck with me: the importance of finding positive role models. If I could look up to him, there were other adult figures out there for me to find and look up to as well. Looking back on it, my role models all had something fantastic in common. They were all people who had found purpose and passion, not only in their jobs and professions, but most important, as caring human beings.

One of the people who stepped into my life along with my uncle was my math teacher in high school, Mr. Shoemaker. He was tall like my uncle but with shoulder-length blond hair, a smart hippie nerd.

He was a quiet man who kept mostly to himself, but when he talked you had to listen or you'd get lost in the dust. He had a dry, witty sense of humor that kept you on your toes.

I bet that nine out of ten of you are probably saying to yourselves, "I hated math. It was torture. I'm glad I don't have to take that again!" But for me it was different. I'm sure a large part of it was that Mr. Shoemaker made learning fun, but math really clicked for me, and I've always seen numbers and their relationships everywhere—phone numbers, addresses, frequent-flyer numbers. It's like a separate language all by itself.

People in music tend to understand the importance of mathematics, because both music and math use the part of the brain that's very analytical and methodical. It's very useful, especially in conducting the business of music. For me, math is my mind's equivalent of going to the gym. It's a workout that gives big results.

Mr. Shoemaker's math class turned out to be a catalyst in some unexpected ways. A major lightbulb went off on my head when Mr. Shoemaker said to the class one day, "If you're looking for a shortcut, there are none. You get out of my class what you put into it. If you want to do better, you have to put in the time. I can't do the work for you. If you have a question, I eat lunch at my desk. I'm here."

When I wasn't in the band room practicing during the lunch hour or out on the quad trying to get up the nerve to talk to the girls in my class, I would be in Mr. Shoemaker's math lab. There was no fooling around or goofing off in there. You came to work. He was there if you needed help. And that was also true outside of the math lab. He made himself available to everyone, not just me. The relationship was there to be had, ripe for the picking. Mr. Shoemaker cared, and he took the time to show us that he did.

He shared this quality with all of the mentors who have shown up in my life, among them Quincy Jones, who you will hear about later. The only thing they required of me was to reach out and say yes to their help, by opening the door to Uncle Frank's car or to Mr. Shoemaker's math lab. The best way I've found to show gratitude to them is to make sure that I'm available to others. When you're truly available and ready, don't worry. The mentors you need will show up and open their world to you.

BLINDED BY ARROGANCE

For much of my teenage life, math for me was an escape, pure and simple. It intrigued me to such a degree that at lunchtime I would often go to the math lab to do my homework because I was so excited. I thought it could also be a way to build my future.

I was already looking ahead to see that working with numbers could be a ticket to a successful adult life.

But, as I soon found out, it is dangerous to get too far ahead of yourself. Math, again, gave me this important lesson. I thought that school was pretty simple. If you showed up for your classes, you would pass. If you paid attention, you could probably ace all your classes.

So, in this state of complacent thinking, I often studied while watching television. More specifically, I studied during the commercials. I was that sure of myself. I hadn't yet learned Mr. Shoemaker's lesson, "The more I learn, the more I learn I need to learn." I hadn't yet had the reality check that would show me that I knew close to nothing in the grand scheme of things.

When I was seventeen years old and a senior in high school, I was taking an advanced calculus class that was especially created for two other students and myself. If I passed this class, I would qualify to take a math course at UCLA once a week for the final semester of my senior year. Not only that, but I would receive a scholarship to UCLA as well. At the end of the advanced calculus class, we had a *take-home* final. I was so cocky, I did my usual thing and watched television as I worked on the test. I was so arrogant, I didn't even bother to go back and check my work. I was getting ahead of myself, way past the finish line.

I came into the class the next day, and Mr. Shoemaker reviewed my final exam. To my shock and dismay, everything was wrong. With mathematic formulas, as with many of life's everyday problems, all you need is for one little number to be off to set off a chain reaction of failure.

Luckily, he gave me a chance to retake the test. My time would be up at the end of the class, a two-hour session set aside for final exams. I was sweating. I knew that I had been in a rush and raced through the test the night before. So I painstakingly started from the beginning, and as I completed each step, I rechecked it to make sure I hadn't gotten it wrong.

Fortunately, I passed the test the second time around and went on to take the class at UCLA during my last semester of high school. I was also accepted to UCLA and qualified for a full scholarship from the Bank of America and Southern California Gas Company, which included tuition, books, and housing expenses, plus a guaranteed summer job, as long as I maintained a 3.0 grade point average. I made it until the middle of my junior year at UCLA, when the opportunities to leave and become a professional musician proved to be too irresistible.

Taking that calculus test was an important moment for me, and it taught me something I have carried with me to every job I've had since. Just when you think you're finished, stop and recheck your work. Because if you don't fine-tune it or at least go over it, chances are huge that you're going to miss something. It's all well and good to be passionate about what you're doing, but don't be blinded by arrogance.

SOMETHING BIGGER AROUND THE CORNER

It seemed that each and every one of the buildings in the Jordan Downs had its very own group of boys trying to emulate the Jackson 5—and our building was no different. We called ourselves the Sensations.

Uncle Frank took an interest in us and started taking us around to various talent shows at the local nightclubs. Our group would have to stay in the back until it was time to perform because we were only twelve years old and couldn't be in an environment where there was drinking. We started winning several amateur competitions, and as a result, we were getting offers to play real gigs and get paid. Our first jobs were at the local military bases.

There was one main thing that set us apart from the competition. My uncle paid for our singing lessons. As part of the instruction, we learned how to do barbershop harmonies. It was an oddity at these talent shows to have a bunch of twelve-year-old kids singing in that style. But that's how and why we won. We would begin our performances by singing along to the Jackson 5 records. It was a no-brainer. They knew we could do that. But for the encore, we'd come out and do five-part harmony, and that gave us an advantage. We weren't just a group that could dance and sing like they expected. We did something completely unexpected.

The Jacksons happened to be the flavor of the month at that time. Name any major artist today, the only way they got in the door was by showing up at an audition and demonstrating how good they were at sounding like Aretha, Whitney, or someone of that stature. Until we had our base, we took a little bit of this and a little bit of that, borrowing from the successful artists who were doing what we wanted to do.

If you're really serious, it will take more than just desire and practice. You will need to be proactive and look out for opportunities to put yourself in an environment where you can learn and grow. Become an apprentice or an intern and be willing to sweep the floors or fetch the coffee if necessary. You can't become a mountain climber unless you're willing to go to the mountain. You may not ultimately become the leader of the company, but what an advantage to work with and learn from the best.

Deer in the Headlights

The Top 24 contestants for American Idol *gather in the television studio where all the magic happens. It's where dreams are made, hearts are broken, and lives are shattered.*

It's the first time that I get the chance to meet them, and they don't quite know it yet, but I will probably be one of the key people in their lives until the competition is complete. Out of the millions who dream about winning American Idol, *the thousands who actually apply, and the weeks of narrowing down finalists at auditions around the country, it always comes down to the "talk."*

Despite the smiles on their faces and the sense of shared excitement at being chosen, there's a palpable tension. Try as they might to hide it, they are nevertheless the proverbial deer in the middle of the road, blinded by the high beams of an oncoming twenty-ton truck. Within a week, they are well aware of the reality. Four of them will already be roadkill! They're totally in awe of everything. The set. Hollywood. Security. Makeup artists. Hairdressers. Cameras. Stage managers. Directors. Segment producers. Video packages. So much information.

Like millions of others around the country, they have watched the show, but this is the real thing. They realize that they will soon get the chance to perform with the same band that has worked with Stevie Wonder, Elton John, Alicia Keys, Sting, Carrie Underwood, and many others. They're listening or trying to listen to what I have to say to them. Part of their success or failure in this beginning stage will come down to who can figure things out the quickest and not get rattled.

Behind their smiles, I know pretty much what they're thinking. It's a mixture of "I'm really good . . . but am I good enough?" "Have my family and friends been kidding me?" "Do I have what it takes?" "Can I even make it to the finals?" Then the last question ultimately is: "Am I the one?"

Idol *is a grand metaphor. Like time-lapse photography of a seedling bursting up through the soil to become a flower,* Idol *encapsulates, compresses, and accelerates, in just a few short weeks, all of the lessons that can otherwise take a lifetime to learn. This is probably one big reason why the show has been such a phenomenon. We see the drama of transformation happening so quickly, right in front of our eyes.*

The most valuable of these fast lessons is how to focus in the eye of the storm. Immediately, the contestants are blinded by the whirlwind of all the heavy, intense activity. When it really starts to swirl, they have to get their footing fast, or else! In ordinary life, most of us only have to deal with not much more than a little dust blowing in the wind.

The millions who watch the show nightly see something in these kids that is a reminder. They look at the contestants and say, "These kids are going after their dreams." It makes some people take a look inside and question, "What am I doing with my life?"

People have the misconception that if you can sing you can become a star. You come in and audition, and the next thing you know you're performing a song on the show. "I can sing.

I'm talented. I can do this!" They go on. "I sing in church. I do weddings. I have my own band."

There's a lot that has to happen between the point where you're singing in the bathroom shower and the place where millions of people know your name. The requirements for excellence are something that amateur singers often take for granted.

So the first thing I do for these twenty-four contestants is to give them "the talk." It is what they call in military jargon a "preemptive strike." With my shaved head, I would look good in one of those Marine Corps drill-sergeant hats.

I begin: "I'm not here to help you win anything. I'm here to make you better. A better person. A better artist. Better, period. There's no mystery here. You get what you give. If you give love and respect, you get it back. You put in hard work and you will reap those rewards.

"At some point your ego is going to rise up, and it's going to pass your talent. For some of you, it's happened already. I would urge you to quickly and quietly put it in check. The minute your ego walks in, God walks out. He's finished. He's finished because you're in control now. He's not going to tussle with you about getting your work done. Your talent is your gift. Now, to further your talent, you've got to put in the work.

"If you're here for the wrong reasons, you will not be successful. Your talent will implode in front of you or totally evaporate. What does not have truth and integrity to it has nothing to feed on but itself. Now you see it, now you don't."

As I finish my remarks and look out at their twenty-four eager faces, I think about the opportunity before them. I don't know how anyone can handle the pressure they're under. What I had to go through in learning the business, as you will read in these pages, was far gentler and infinitely more merciful.

The whole world wasn't watching me. I was groomed over time by the school of hard knocks. I can't offer them any such luxury.

The Idol *process will always be challenging, and at times, unforgiving. Everyone wants to win. To have a chance, they will have to do more than please the judges and the American public. To survive, they will have to conquer their own heavy internal obstacles step by step—what I call the breakthroughs.*

PART TWO

Testing the Waters

NEVER TOO EARLY TO INVEST

Once the Sensations started getting attention, our next step was to get a band. We went to the local high school and found young musicians to be in our backing band. Uncle Frank had returned from Vietnam and was working full-time as a computer programmer at an aerospace and defense company called Rockwell. He spent the weekends working with us on our dream.

So there I was, thirteen years old and singing in a band with these high school musicians. We were being hired for jobs and making money. But by the summer of that year, the high school musicians all graduated and didn't want to play with kids anymore. Uncle Frank said, "I've run out of young local musicians. I've gone to all the schools in the area. You guys are going to have to learn how to play your own instruments." Since I was singing Jermaine Jackson's part, it was obvious to me that I should learn the instrument that he played. That's why I became a bass player. Now it was time for us to take private lessons again, but this time with instruments.

In six months' time, the other members of the group started losing interest in the music lessons. I was the only one who stayed with it. I had a notebook, and every time I learned a new song, I would write down the names of its title and performer in my book: "Skin Tight," by the Ohio Players. "Play That Funky Music," by Wild Cherry. I sat by the radio with my bass, and when they came on, I'd play along with the radio. A few months later, Uncle Frank stopped by for a visit and I showed him my notebook, which by then contained more than a hundred songs. "Hey, look at this," I told him. "I'm ready to start a band. Will you manage us?" He said yes, and with that, became the manager of my new band, called Potential.

We saved the money we made from our performances and opened a checking and savings account. Uncle Frank had already taught me how to invest in the first band. The Sensations had recycled the earnings to pay for our first instruments and our music lessons. With the new band, we took it to a higher level. We bought a van, sound system, drum set, bass and guitar amplifier, a Stradivarius trumpet, and a new high-end microphone for the singer. When the business side of things came together, we had the foundation to focus on the creative: practicing, learning, and putting in the time to get better. There's no creativity without economic stability. You can't just go after your dreams and not eat. Someone has to believe in you and finance it. And who's better to believe in you than you?

I played the clarinet in the school marching band. But all that changed when I walked by the choir room at school one day. For some reason I walked in, and the choir teacher, Ms. Payne, said to me, "Hey, some of the kids tell me you play bass. We need a bass player for the choir." Soon I was performing with the choir. She also suggested that I start playing at various churches. That was an education in itself. You can learn so much working with a gospel choir. They have proven to be the breeding ground for some of the most inspirational singers in the world.

The traditional songs in most Baptist churches are derived from hymns and old Negro spirituals. Gospel is also infused with an exciting mix of elements and influences from blues, jazz, and R & B. Not only did I get all of that in one setting, but the icing on the cake was the heavenly voices that made us forget all the worries of the day.

Another benefit of playing in the school choir was that it got me out of physical education classes. "This is cool. You mean I don't have to go to gym?"

Back with my first group, the Sensations, we weren't the best singers, and we weren't the best dancers. But we stood out because we tried to do something different. Now, with Potential, we applied the same formula. There were people who played better than we did. But we were the complete package. We had the choreography. We had the lighting. We had great pacing. Our songs sounded fresh.

We looked sharp in our snazzy stage outfits. When we weren't wearing our white outfits, we had polyester leisure suits in bold blue or lime. We made up big canvas banners to hang on the wall behind us with the word POTENTIAL color-coordinated to match our costumes.

The road I chose happened to be music, but it could've just as easily been a lemonade stand. I think I always felt that if I pushed a little harder and did a little extra there would be something bigger around the corner.

STAY ON YOUR BIKE

Some of the friends that I rode bikes with as a kid never ventured very far out of the neighborhood later in life. Some might even have been near misses, but it's a cruel fact of life that for myriad reasons the deck was stacked against them. I've seen it happen many times in my work. Why is it that an artist will work very hard, write great songs, get a record deal, go into the studio, make the album, and then, poof, everything disappears?

You won't get anywhere in this world without determination and perseverance, especially when things don't go your way. Get used to it. Those qualities will be tested frequently. You have to keep asking yourself, "How badly do I want this?"

But in order to find the strength to accomplish your goals, you have to be willing to take a journey inward first. The truth of the matter is that every time you try to expand your boundaries, whether you're taking your first baby steps or already far along the road, your attitudes and beliefs about yourself can end up being your toughest obstacles. I've seen the enemy, and it's the person staring right back at me in the mirror. To go beyond your comfort zone, you can't have any chinks in your body armor of self-love and confidence. If you do, your insecurities and fears of pain and disappointment will find ingenious ways to grind you to a halt.

I realize that with this advice I'm not saying anything profound or anything that you haven't heard before. But because I see this problem of self-doubt rearing its ugly head at almost every curve in the road, it bears repeating.

What's behind our fear of success? "My mother thinks I'm good." Friends say, "You should go on *American Idol.*" Co-workers tell you, "I'd vote for you. You'd win." But in the back of your mind, you're saying, "Can I do it?" For every person who tries out for *American Idol*, there are probably hundreds who talk themselves out of trying. It's the same with any competition. We ask ourselves, "What's the use? There can only be one first baseman on the team. What if I don't even make the team? Can I handle the rejection?"

That little voice of self-doubt doesn't just come out of nowhere. It has the uncanny ability to speak up right when you're at a decisive fork in the road. As a young child, maybe you were told you were not good enough by a parent, caregiver, or teacher. Or it could have been something said on the playground. Someone might have told you scornfully, "You're never going to make it," as if there were a photo of you in your high school yearbook with the caption "Most likely *not* to succeed." Again, you may know in your logical mind that what was said about you was not true, but that little voice can still stick around in your subconscious mind and create havoc.

So I understand how and why it can feel easier and safer to get off the bike and not go any farther. Just to clarify, staying on the bike doesn't imply that you just ride, ride, ride into the glorious sunset and don't ever get off. No, staying on the bike means you ride, fall, get up, ride, slip, get up, ride, fix the flat tire, get up, ride. . . .

There are many times when I've been knocked off my bike, and I thought in the heat of the moment that I would never get back on. Yes, almost all of those circumstances were my own doing. My feelings got hurt. Someone said something or did something to me, and I took it personally. I thought I was being disrespected, and I was ready to quit, hand in my notice. I'll show you all! Revenge is mine! "You'll miss me when I'm gone."

And the truth is, they might miss me, but I would end up unemployed and the show would still go on. We all have to understand that. As important as we think we are, we are all replaceable. So, in your journey, as you're finding your way, know that with every job that you get, every business that you own, any venture can be gone in the blink of an eye.

Whether you're at the beginning of your road, or a bit farther along, keep in mind that many of the issues that you have to deal with when you're starting out may repeat themselves later in life. This is why I'm jumping ahead in the chronology to tell a story that drives home my point of how easily replaceable we are when we let our negative emotions run the show.

At this point in my career, I had held the post of music director for a major artist for two years, but you could still consider me a beginner when it came to realizing what I'm about to tell you. The meat of this story was that we were about to go out on a new tour. I thought, all things being equal, that I deserved a raise. I had worked hard. I had proven myself. I looked around at how much money they were spending on the tour. I looked at how much they were making on the tickets and the merchandising. They had just added twice as many lights. They had these expensive tour buses and trucks. "Hey, I'm doing some heavy lifting here," I thought to myself. But the problem was that I had already accepted the job and agreed to the terms. So I went ahead and put in for a raise.

When I came in to get the decision, the manager immediately gave me a piece of paper with the total amount that I would make during the tour, and said. "Now, this is what you're willing to walk away from?" He didn't even bother to address why I'd asked for the raise. He said, "Here's the amount of money that you're going to make on this tour. You're saying that you want more than this, and that if you don't get it, you're going to walk away. Do I understand you clearly?"

Well, just for the record, the rule here is if you ask for a raise, you should be prepared for them to say no and get ready to pack your belongings. One other word for the wise: You won't get a raise if you're wishy-washy and say, *Dear Sir, maybe, if it's OK, can I get a few dollars more? If not, never mind, I don't want to make you mad and cause you to fire me.* . . .

So I wanted a raise. And they said "no." So we were at a stalemate. I thought, "You know what, they need me. They're not going to let me go." I had started rehearsals. I'd already accepted the deal, and here I was trying to renegotiate. I wanted more. This went on for a week. The tension was really uncomfortable between myself, the artist, and management. I was ready to throw in the towel, thinking, "I could still get a job at IBM. I don't need this. They don't appreciate me. They don't respect me."

Then it hit me. After a week of sleepless nights, I said to myself, "How much is enough?" Imagine if they turned around and said, "We'll pay you double or triple." Would I be happy then? Would I be satisfied? The answer was that I would never feel like I was getting enough because there would always be more to get. So I had to ask myself, "Are you getting paid fairly?" The answer was yes. I think we all feel that we should get more, and that we deserve more. I don't know anybody who says, "I'm making too much money. Can you reduce my salary?"

In this case, you can see how easy it is to be your own worst enemy. Forget about what the rest of the competition is doing to us compared to the nonsense we serve up for ourselves. It's not personal unless you make it so, and I had been ready to jump off the bike and burn it. My emotions had taken over in place of good common sense. I didn't get the raise. I went back and told them that I was fine with the deal we had. It released me from the bondage of my brain droning on with this obsession about getting what I deserved, like an old phonograph record with its needle stuck on a speck of dust. I wasn't going to hold on to bitterness and anger.

To get around these kinds of self-defeating actions, we have to dig deep inside, recognize and acknowledge how our past has affected us, and grow from it. Sometimes, we need a therapist to help us uncover the roots of our actions because we have repressed certain feelings for so long. We may have chosen to deflect the hurt, pain, and disappointment of our pasts by pointing the finger of fault at someone or something else. We use excuses and blame: "I would be better if this happened . . . if that happened. . . . If my mom had been able to afford to keep me in lessons, I'd be a better musician."

Why did I ask for the raise and what did it reveal about me? Here was my rationale: I thought that I had done an excellent job for the two years I had been the music director. My original salary was established when the client didn't know what I could do, and I didn't know what the job entailed. At this point, I had now proven my worth, but I had also learned that the job required a lot more of me than I envisioned in the beginning. I wanted to be in the driver's seat to determine my own value. By saying "no" to my demand, they were telling me, "You are going as fast as the traffic will allow." I wanted to be out of the pack, and I wasn't quite at that level. The truth was that I was being paid well and at fair market value. Instead, my ego had wanted some greater form of acknowledgment, recognition, and respect for my good work, not realizing that the act of being asked back was sufficient by itself. A lot of people get invited, but not everyone gets invited back. It was a valuable lesson. The fact that I got so upset about this situation told me I had some work to do from the inside.

If you have love and self-confidence in your heart, you will rarely let anything that anybody says about you deter you. And most important, you won't let your own negative attitudes defeat you. You will be ready to take more control over your destiny.

Don't be discouraged by the fact that not everyone is meant to be a leader. We can't all be the chief, the supervisor, the boss, the president, or the owner. Not everyone achieves the goals they set. But the journey of reaching for them is an equally important part of the process. If you don't go, you won't grow. The late singer-songwriter Oscar Brown, Jr. said it best: "I may not make it if I try, but I damn sure won't if I don't." Get back up on your bike. Keep pedaling.

THE DUST ON TOP OF THE REFRIGERATOR

There was a notice on the bulletin board at the UCLA recreation center saying that jazz musician Nat Adderley was going to give a lunchtime lecture. Even though I was on a math scholarship at UCLA, I was still clearly interested in music. The talk fit perfectly between my classes. I didn't know much about the trumpeter other than one fact. Someone had once given me a Cannonball Adderley record, and I knew that Nat was his brother and frequent collaborator. Cannonball played on some of the historic albums with Miles Davis that revolutionized jazz in the late 1950s. It all sounded good, so I signed up for the lecture.

Some people claim they find clarity by fasting for forty days. Similarly, others espouse the value of traveling. Both may be true, but my experience is that often the pearls of wisdom are right in front of us all the time. The key to uncovering them, I think, starts with being willing to make that first step. Seeing that notice on the bulletin board and deciding to give up my lunch break is one such example in my life.

Think about it. Where does your inspiration come from? It could be looking at a flower or reading a quote from a philosopher or poet. But whatever the source, inspiration comes to us only because we are open and available to look for it. It is like that mystical experience of randomly opening up to a page in a book and discovering a passage that perfectly fits your life situation that day.

The inspiration I got that day happened to come to me in the form of that notice on the bulletin board. Most of the time, these things are right under our noses, if we choose to see them. You can stop this second, not after you're done with this book, but right now, and take advantage of a lot of opportunities to help you move forward in your life. That day it happened to be the bulletin board at school, but had I stopped and had a word with my professor at the end of class, it might have had the same effect, offering some information that would inspire me, encourage me, and thrust me forward.

Surrounding yourself with inspiration can be a simple and powerful exercise. If there's a song that inspires you, keep it close to you. Whenever you feel down, listen to that song. If there's a physical place that gives you inspiration, go there and get a clean start.

But don't get stuck thinking that these moments of realization have to hit you like a bolt of lightning. Sometimes we have to store inspiration away like a good bottle of vintage wine and let it mature. Most of the time we don't really "get it" right away.

I went into the classroom and was immediately surprised that it wasn't that crowded. Even though I didn't know much about Nat Adderley, there was something about him that was intriguing. I couldn't quite put my finger on it as I sat there listening to this old guy talking about his experience in music.

He asked the audience, "How many of you people like jazz?"

There was a resounding cheer from the thirty students—"*Yeahhhh!!!*"

This was a small but lively group.

He said, "That's great. How many of you love rock?"

"*Yeah!*" Not quite as loud as before.

"I'm going to play a couple of things for you."

He put a vinyl record on the turntable. Then he wanted to know whether we liked it. There was a vote by hands. "So, the majority of you didn't like this piece of music. Let's talk about that. Why didn't you like it?" A person stood up and answered, echoing what most of the rest of us in the audience were thinking as well.

"I don't know. It just sounded like somebody banging on pots and pans. The horn player seemed like he was just playing random notes. It didn't seem to really matter what key."

Nat responded, "I'm going to share something with you that my brother taught me. He said to me one day many years ago, 'This cat's coming down from Kansas City. They call him "Bird." This cat can put down some sounds.' So I decided to

29

meet up with Cannonball and check it out." Nat was talking about going to see the legendary Charlie Parker perform.

"I got to the club and sat down. Bird was playing. And a short time later, I walked out. I caught up with Cannonball later that night at a jam session. He said, 'Man, where'd you go?' I said, 'Man, that was nothing but noise. That ain't music.' He said, 'You know the problem with you? You don't like it because you don't understand it. You don't know enough about this style of playing to understand and appreciate it. I'm not saying that it has to be your favorite style of music. But you're ignorant. You're ignorant to what he's doing.'"

Nat Adderley went on to tell us that once we truly understood the music we had just heard, our appreciation would go up. He reiterated what his brother had said, that everything we listen to will not be our favorite piece, but we should learn to recognize and appreciate what goes into it: the artistry, the talent, the craft, and all the various nuances.

Then it hit me. Just a year earlier, Mr. Henry Grant, the owner of the music school I attended, had given me an album that I remember playing for what I deemed would be the first and the last time. I immediately disliked it, and I had banished it to the top of the refrigerator in the little guesthouse in Watts that I rented.

After the lecture by Nat Adderley, I went home and found the album where I had left it, covered in thick dust from a year of neglect. Charlie Mingus's *Mingus, Mingus, Mingus*. I put it on. The first song I listened to was "Better Git It In Your Soul." The title felt like an omen. It proved to be more of a godsend.

How strange that my feelings about it would turn on a dime because I happened to go to that luncheon lecture. The day before, the album was doomed, dead and buried in my mind as something that was clearly not fit for my ears. To this day, I can sing all of the parts of the orchestra, the drums, the bass, and the horns. Suddenly, I discovered what a phenomenal arranger Mingus was. I listened to it differently this time for one main reason. I had made a major attitude shift.

It can be much easier to dismiss something as bad rather than doing the work to dig down a bit deeper and understand it. When you find yourself not wanting to open up and try something, maybe it's because you haven't been willing to do your research in order to understand the possibilities.

You may still be saying "I hate math. . . . What does math have to do with anything? . . . Why am I still taking this class? . . . Why do I have to solve some word problem about how much wine is consumed in Italy?"

I don't mean this only as a message to young people, but to older people as well. Whether we are just starting out or have been around the block a few times, we all become set in our ways and routines. We want control, so we don't willingly invite change into our world.

The Charlie Mingus album was a challenge to me to move out of my complacency, a brisk slap in the face. It was as if a doorway had magically opened once I was willing to take that album on and learn to appreciate it. The next level was waiting. It taught me as well that at the moment you're about to have a breakthrough, there is usually some accompanying discomfort (and, most definitely, some hard work). No pain, no gain.

Sure you can say, "Well, you just didn't know enough music. That's why you couldn't appreciate the Mingus album." That was certainly true. But the other part of the equation is something that we don't always want to admit. That is, not only do we not know enough, but we may not be *ready*. Remember, that record gathered dust on top of my refrigerator for good reason. That's OK. Don't think that when opportunity comes, and you're shut down, ignorant, or just not ready for it, that it's always a bad thing. You shouldn't get down on yourself about that. Instead, what's most important is *recognizing* that you were not ready for the opportunity—and then asking yourself, "What do I need to do to get ready for it? There was something about this thing that I didn't like. What was it?"

Just acknowledging that you're not ready may not mean that you will ever be ready. But when you make the effort to understand and appreciate something new, it opens you up to having a more expressive palate and a broader range of experiences.

Perhaps part of your challenge with all of this is that you simply have no idea where your passion lies or what you should be doing to find it. You may even be questioning why you're here on this earth. "I'm not good at anything. I can't do anything well." For some, this sort of self-doubt is a self-fulfilling prophecy. You were once told that you're not good at anything, and that's what you believe. That's one side of the problem. The other part deals with the rut we create for ourselves, our attachment to keeping things just as they are, both the good and bad. This tendency is obvious in people who prefer to stay in abusive relationships, for example: When we fear change, we often choose to remove ourselves from the daily stream of opportunities for growth. This avoidance can show its face in many forms of addiction and distraction that you will read about later on. I would say to those who haven't quite figured out what they want out of life to just go out and experiment.

There's no way you'll find out unless you're willing to stick your neck out a bit and try something new. Here's the kicker: In truth, it's far easier to venture out and discover what you love to do and what you're great at than it is to let go of the old patterns that are holding you back. How easy it could have been for me to let things stay in the status quo. Charlie Mingus would still be collecting dust.

NO SHAME IN BEING GREEN

I got a call on a Wednesday night. The voice on the other end was music conductor Victor O. Hall. He said, "We got your number from session drummer Ndugu Chancellor." He got quickly to the point. "We're looking for a bass player. We leave Friday morning. We're flying to Newport News, Virginia, and Bloomington, Minnesota." I was twenty years old and had already left college. I had never been on a plane before. This was my first real professional gig. I was about to hit the road with Gladys Knight and the Pips, the legendary Motown group best known for "I Heard It Through the Grapevine" and later for "Midnight Train to Georgia," among dozens of classic hits.

"You'll need a tuxedo. We'll give you the sheet music when you get there."

I went right away to the thrift store and bought a tuxedo for about five dollars. I also got three tuxedo shirts for a buck each. I was thinking ahead. Those would last me for the trip because I wouldn't have time or money for the hotel laundry. I also needed a pair of black shoes. I got a few other things at the thrift store, since it was, after all, wintertime, and it would be cold where I was going. I had checked the weather forecast in the newspaper, and it said that it would be snowing in Minnesota. Before I left the store, I purchased one of those lumberjack hats with the furry earflaps and a pair of used snow boots.

Lastly, the store had a good selection of used luggage, and I didn't have a suitcase because I had never gone anywhere before—so I bought two pieces. At the cash register, I put all of my new pre-owned items in the suitcases.

Friday morning, and I'm on the plane. I must have looked a sight. I was sitting in my seat with all of my winter gear on. I've got my hat on with the earflaps down and tied under my chin. I've got my snow boots on. I'm sitting there, listening to everything that the flight attendant has to say. I'm doing everything to a T—I've got my seat belt fastened correctly and I've practiced putting my head between my legs in case of a crash. I am not making this up. I don't know what I was thinking, but it's probably because I was green as hell. A couple of hours later, when we change planes, I notice some of the other members of the band snickering and making gestures like "this guy is weird with that hat on." To add to the drama, I had also packed my ticket for our connecting flight in my checked bag. So the road manager had to buy me a new ticket.

Now, at our final destination, we're at the baggage claim. I meet Gladys for the first time. She'd come in on another plane from another location. We're all waiting, and everyone has his or her baggage except for me. Then, finally, out comes that last suitcase. "Who's is this?" they asked me. "It's mine." They look at me like I'm from another planet. How was I to know that I'd bought a woman's vanity case? Hey, I thought, it had a mirror in it, it's small, and I can put lots of things in it, including my toiletries. Needless to say, I got a crash education in traveling, wardrobe, and luggage that day.

But how quickly things change. As soon as we got out of the airport and stepped outside into the weather, everybody started slipping and sliding. Everybody, that is, except me. I might have looked silly. But like a good Boy Scout, I was prepared.

A few days later, I came to this realization: "Just think. I'm on tour and on the bus with Gladys and these great musicians. I'm playing my bass." It hit me for the very first time. I looked at the itinerary. I saw the list with hotel room assignments. Gladys Knight's and my name are on the same list. "I can actually do this for a living."

I pictured myself traveling the world and playing, and soon I would be. I was blown away by the fact that I could be in Japan playing with a horn player who didn't speak English, and yet we had this common language of music. I could suddenly see the payoff for all the hard work I had done, all the hours and hours of study and practice.

I was just so happy to be a working musician. I couldn't understand why people were complaining. About wanting more money, about wanting anything! I'm playing this wooden thing with metal strings and electronics in it. They're paying me. They're covering my hotel room, plus an allowance for food. There are people who chauffeur us around in limos and vans. I must have died and gone to heaven. What are they all complaining about?

I did a lot of other things a beginner might do while touring with Gladys and the Pips. I learned quickly the discipline of the road after staying out all night one time. I did it for a silly reason: "Because I could." I paid for it the next day by being way off my game, and I never did it again. Other mistakes also had immediate consequences. Even if we were at a hotel for just one night, I would unpack all my clothes and put them into the dresser and put my shoes under the bed—and then I would often forget and leave them behind for the next guest. If we went to an exciting place like London, I would knock on everybody's doors early in the morning to try to get them to go sightseeing with me. Their faces weren't so friendly. That's what you do when you're green.

Being around all those people on the road, you find out what's important to you. There are times when you want to be in the group and hang out with everyone, and times when you need to step back and spend some time alone, away from the chaos and distractions. On the road, I also learned quickly what to do and what not to do. Both the positive and the negative worked as my teacher. If I showed up late, there were consequences for that or any other kind of bad behavior. All those things that my grandmother used to say to me as a small child were suddenly right on the money.

"Kindness will take you further than money" reminded me always that if I was sincere and genuine, everyone would help me—from the bellman, to the housekeepers, to the other musicians, and so on. "God don't like ugly, and he ain't too crazy about pretty" would stop me from having a fit if I didn't like something. And "All that glitters is not gold" (from the international standardized version of the grandmother how-to book) was self-explanatory. Nothing is what it seems.

That first week, I remember sitting in the pit and seeing all the musicians in the orchestra, the horns and strings. The other members of the band noticed that I was able to sight-read the music charts, and that impressed them. When we were on the bus, the others would always see me with my headphones on, listening and studying various styles of music. They saw that I was focused and noticed that I was getting better. I was pretty serious but also silly, not above putting whoopee cushions under their butts. I was still only twenty. I was on the road with guys who were older and had seen it all. Most of them were married with children.

When I first committed to becoming a full-time musician shortly before joining Gladys and the Pips, I would go to the rehearsal rooms at the Musicians Union Local 47 on Vine Street in Hollywood, a place known to every working musician in L.A., whether you were a big star or played Bar Mitzvahs. It was part labor exchange, part social club. The old-timers were often there playing cards and giving advice. "Hey, little fellow, you must be doing something right. They're talking about you. Remember not everyone is willing to put in the work that you're doing. You've got to know that if you keep pushing, you're going to be leaving your friends behind. It's going to be one of the hardest things."

Gladys Knight and the Pips and the rest of the band eventually looked at me as a dedicated musician. They sensed that this gig was not the end-station for me. I wanted to have other experiences and learn as much as possible beyond this one gig. Things started to shift little by little, and without pushing anything, I eased the band into studying more music. Before long and very spontaneously, this young green kid was inspiring the whole band to reconnect with their passion for learning music.

I just put it out there, thinking if they want it, they'll find it. They'll gravitate to it. And they did. It was humbling and inspiring for me. These musicians, who I had put up on a pedestal, showed me that no matter how big you get, there's always something to learn. This was hardly the end of the story. Even though I had dumped the earflaps and the vanity case, I was still green and had plenty more lessons to learn.

PAY YOUR DUES FIRST

Right after we came off a series of tour dates, Gladys was going into the studio to record a new album. Nathan East, a session bass player who had also recommended me for the touring gig, said, "Look, I won't be able to make all of the sessions because I'm taking flying lessons. So, you should let Rickey do it. He's a good bass player. He can read music." It was my first foray into doing a session with all the big guys. Wow! I would get to play with all these top musicians who have played on thousands of records. So I went in. The first day was a triple session, meaning three recording sessions packed into one day. (Session one ran from ten A.M. to one P.M. This was followed by lunch and then the second session from two P.M. to five P.M., which in turn was followed by dinner. The final session of the day ran from six P.M. until nine.) I got there early and sat down next to Nathan. I was like a fly on the wall. I watched all the musicians as they prepared for each song. They were so good they didn't even look at the music charts until it was time to count off the song and record. I eagerly put on a pair of headphones and listened to how they made the music magically come alive. I asked myself, "If this ain't livin', I don't know what is."

I started playing after the dinner break at six P.M. It was getting close to nine, and we hadn't even finished the one song in this session. There was a lot of discord between the songwriter, the arranger, Gladys, and the engineer. Everybody was trying to figure out how to make this song work. Soon, the musicians were tired. We had one last shot to try to get it right.

The song began with a part that was slow. The band would then start up on cue after Gladys sang a certain line. I thought, "I've played with Gladys. I understand what she's trying to tell the band to do." So I decided to step up and say, "I know what she wants to happen." When Gladys heard what I recommended, she said to the other musicians, "Just follow Rickey." Keep in mind, I'm twenty-one now, and I'm there with all the legend cats. This is my shining moment. We started the song. She did her line and then I came right in. Bam! I started playing. I looked around. Not a single guy was playing. Gladys turned around to me and said, "I thought you knew where I was going." It was at that moment that I realized I had made a big mistake. I had heard the expression before: "You've got to pay your dues." But now I understood it. Those guys showed me.

"Look, kid. We're going into overtime. If we do, it's going to make us more money. Don't try to come in here and be Superman and save the day." They pointed through the glass. "They are the producers. Let them figure it out." They did not want me to try to be the hero.

You can't come into a new situation and try to fix things unless you know all the details of what transpired before you got there. Chances are that someone has already thought of whatever you're suggesting. Instead, you might want to politely ask if they've tried it before.

After that first long night in the studio, I made it standard operating procedure to take a brief moment and step back to observe the room when entering a new situation and certainly before opening my big trap.

I learned a second, more specific set of lessons in "dues paying" several months later. I decided after doing a few road trips with Gladys that I would stay in L.A. for a while with a regular gig. I heard there was an opening for a bass player in the orchestra at the Shubert Theater for the Broadway production of *Dreamgirls*. I auditioned and got the job. It was great pay, with union benefits.

When I met the orchestra for the first time, it was clear to them that I was the new kid off the road. A few of them took me aside and gave me the rules. Eugene "Snooky" Young was the first. He played the trumpet and was known for his mastery of the plunger mute. He also worked with the *Tonight Show* Band for twenty-five years.

He said, "Hey, little fellow, I've been watching you. You're doing the right thing. You're the first person down here in the orchestra pit. You're studying the music. You keep to yourself. Don't let those other guys try to intimidate you."

There were others in the orchestra who also gave me tips. They said, "Don't just show up on time—come early." "Don't be the last one into the pit—be the first." "Keep your attitude and your ego in check." They told me how complaining and egomania are like contagious diseases. "You need to remove yourself from people like that," they said. True to their advice, I saw right away how some musicians were working themselves right out of a job because of their bad attitude. They thought they were better than everybody else. They used the act of putting other people down to try to push themselves up.

They went on. "It's okay to make suggestions, but do it in a way that people will hear. Don't come off like you're telling someone what to do."

And last but not least, some down-to-earth practical advice: "Don't go out and make an expensive purchase just because of this paycheck. The show could close tomorrow. None of this lasts forever."

HOLD ON TIGHT TO YOUR SOUL

Remember what I told the *Idol* contestants about making sure they were there for all the right reasons? Best to do a gut check right from the start. Like my math final exam, a mistake not remedied in the beginning can prove to be your undoing.

It makes good common sense that if you don't have a positive motivation driving you, you have a recipe for trouble. It will be sure to catch up with you as your career develops and your relationships become more complicated. Unless your head (and your heart) are perfectly clear in this regard, it's easy to become distracted and create chaos. You may become bitter and disappointed or let things become too personal.

OK, that sounds great. But do you want the truth? Did I have some big motivation when I was a young kid starting out? Honestly, here's where my head was at the time:

I got money. Girls are interested.

Somewhat narrow in scope? Yes. Positive? Well, that depends on your interpretation. Of course, my mentality was hardly much different from that of any other teenager at the time. Luckily, my vistas soon expanded, and I moved on to more mature goals.

All of us need to make periodic attitude adjustments. If you don't change the oil in your car, don't expect things to run smoothly in the long run. But some people just don't get it. They ignore the nasty smoke coming out of their exhaust pipes. Here are some examples:

CASE #1: Everybody who works for this one very famous artist is unanimous in saying that he is a very unhappy person. They all say, "You should have met him before he was successful. He was a happy guy." The greater his success, the nastier he became. He went through four or five marriages, numerous breakups of his groups and bands—each collapse made him darker and darker.

CASE #2: I recently played at a gig accompanying one of the former contestants from *Idol*. Think about it. A few years earlier, I had spent several weeks in close daily contact with this person. At the bare minimum, we had some history together that was worth something. But cut to the situation at hand. It was time for the performance. What did this person choose to do? This artist totally ignored us. Unbelievable. It was as if the band members and myself were invisible. All it would have taken was a look across the stage in our direction, a nod, a wink, or a wave. A "nice to see you guys again" could have done the trick. Musicians are like elephants. They don't forget.

CASE #3: This is about another hugely successful guy. He's written some of the biggest songs, a performer and musician known the world over. He needs no introduction. Yet the monkey on his back has to do with his inability to communicate with others. It's not that he isn't a nice person. He just isn't consistent in articulating what he wants. Where he goes, chaos follows. It's amazing that he's able to get the kind of work and respect that he gets. Drama kings and queens apparently thrive in chaos.

Maybe this last person has ADD. And the former *Idol* contestant could be hiding some pain from the past. The first one is anyone's guess. That said, in my work, I really don't have the luxury of time or the qualifications to sit around psychoanalyzing everybody and everything. I've got work to do. If a problem comes up, as you will read later on in several examples, I deal with it head-on and try to find a solution.

In the same way, if your attitude starts creating problems for you, you need to take action. The right help is always close at hand if you are open to receiving it. The people I've told you about may be laughing all the way to the bank, but the negative issues they are creating for everyone around them are no joke. It's tragic to look back at how a lifetime of trauma and suffering could have been prevented, both for these types of people and those within radar range.

If you're building your business, but you've sold everyone down the river and damaged all your relationships, is that really the kind of life you want to have? Being successful financially is one thing, but think about all the bad karma and toxic load that people like that carry around.

It all comes down to the kind of life you want to live. They can say, "I'm totally fine with it. I'm fine with barreling through and running all over people." Their motto is, "Whatever it takes, I will do. Even if it means selling my soul."

Most successful people in the music business, no matter how big they become, carry inside of them a spirit of appreciation and gratitude for the opportunities they've been given. That aspect alone helps to create positive energy around them. If you have that, too, you will reap all kinds of benefits, not the least of which is having very enjoyable relationships and a good night's sleep.

HOW TO AGE TEN YEARS IN ONE DAY

This has happened to me and to so many other musicians that it can almost be considered a rite of passage. And I'm sure there is an equivalent version in almost any job. I hope that by reading this story it prevents you from the stress and needless suffering of this all-too-common situation.

It starts off innocently enough and with positive intentions, but then turns really ugly. I was young and just starting out on the music circuit. The good word was getting out, and I was getting multiple job offers. I was so grateful for this, and the last thing I wanted to do was to disappoint anybody. I had the disease to please. When the phone rang, I would almost invariably say yes and take the job, unless I had a *direct* scheduling conflict. Perhaps there was also the naive fear inside that if I told them no, maybe they would never call back. What if the phone stopped ringing altogether?

Believe it or not, it is humanly possible to get fired from three jobs in one day. It almost happened to me. The first of these was playing in a band for a Sunday brunch. Things were going so well that the owner of the restaurant asked the bandleader how much it would cost to extend the set by an hour. The bandleader was thrilled and made the deal without bothering to consult any of us. We would each get an extra $50.

That effectively took care of the one hour of travel time I had planned for to arrive and get set up for the next gig. But it went on even longer. I looked down at my watch. It had gone over an additional five minutes. Tick-tock. Suddenly, it was fifteen minutes. "I've got to go," I told the bandleader while unplugging my bass from the amplifier. "Then take your s**t and leave," he barked back at me. As I was packing the rest of my gear away, he really lit into me. How tired he was of greedy young kids!

He even did the "back in the day" rap about how no one in Count Basie's or Duke Ellington's orchestra would dare to pull that kind of stunt.

I rushed to the next gig, but they had already started playing without me. I had to walk through the audience to get to the stage. Trust me, the memory of that sort of embarrassment does not fade with the passing years. To all the members of that band watching me walk across the room with my gear, I was another young kid making a bad name for himself.

The last job was supposed to start at nine P.M. I got there at 9:30. They had not started. They had waited for me. I don't know if that fact made matters better or worse. I had made everybody late. Bottom line, they were pissed at me. Very pissed.

So, that extra $50 set off a domino effect. The whole spectacle made me look like a bad person, just in it for the money and as silly as a dog chasing its tail. I tried to make everybody happy and succeeded in totally infuriating each and every one of them.

As an employer, I've had to fire some who followed in my foolish footsteps. Here is what they had in common with me: They wanted to do a good job. They wanted to be on time. They wanted to honor their commitment. But they also wanted to do every job that came in.

All it takes is for one thing to go wrong, and then the situation degenerates quickly from wishful thinking, to poor planning, to huge stress, and finally, to disaster. The right intentions may be there, but the law of averages will catch up with you and demand its due. A car crash and a traffic jam are just a few of the normal things that can and will go wrong. And as a result, when you end up unable to honor your commitments, people will say, "I'm not going to use him again—he's late all the time. He's not true to his word."

It's OK to accept that second job, but there has to be full disclosure when you are booking things tightly. I'm impressed when someone I'm hiring is open with me: "Hey, I have another job. I have an hour in between. I think I can make it. I just want to let you know. So if you're not comfortable, you can call someone else and have them do it." That way, it becomes my choice. I might tell that person, "I'm willing to take that chance because you add something special to the project that's worth it."

I understand the reasons for wanting to work and never refusing an opportunity. But please heed my warning about taking on more than you can handle, especially those of you who consider yourselves smart and ambitious. You're far from immune to the temptation. The laws of physics still say that you can be in only one place at one time. Hey, if Quincy Jones could magically have been at every place that wanted him, I would have never gotten a job.

THE FINE ART OF SCREWING UP

While we're on the subject of making big mistakes, let's talk strategy for a second. This will come in handy for you sooner rather than later, I promise you.

I'm an authority on this subject because I make mistakes all the time. My blunders range from mundane slipups to horrible days when I tell the band to go home, crawl into bed, and wait for a new day. OK, the deed has been done, but what can you do to lessen its impact? File the following advice away in an accessible place for use whenever damage control is necessary.

Let's begin with a multiple-choice question. The producer wanted me to change an arrangement a certain way, and I didn't do it. Now he's asking me why I didn't. What should I do?

I reply to the producer:

A. I didn't get your e-mail and my voice mail was full.
B. I'm sorry. I overslept and there was an accident on the freeway.
C. I don't remember you saying that.

Any one of those answers might just be correct. In fact, the mistake you made may not be completely your fault.

NONE OF THIS MATTERS. It's really futile to sit there and make excuses for what wasn't done. Or start playing the blame game. The most prudent use of your time is to own up to the mistake. The thing that matters is, *can you fix it?*

People want solutions. You're either part of the problem or part of the solution. Figure out which side you're on. If your boss comes in and says to you, "This is all wrong," your correct response should be, "It will be done right away." No excuses. Don't bother with a long-winded, defensive "this is what happened." It's a waste of time. Get to the solution.

While you're at it, make sure to also give them your time frame for solving the problem. You're not only saying you'll do it, but also *when* it will be done. The last thing my producer wants to hear is, "I'll get to it in a few days."

I know right now your ego may be saying, "Yes, but." We'll get around to that discussion in a moment. Here's the method to the madness: You might have the greatest excuse in the world. But when you own up to the mistake, it totally defuses the situation.

I decided a long time ago to be the thermostat and not the thermometer. If someone came to me in a heated rage, upset and out of control, I didn't want to add more fuel to the fire. Instead, I wanted them to come down to my cooler temperature. So, when dealing with heat that can boil water (212 degrees Fahrenheit, to be exact), I say, "No problem, I'll get to it right away." Then I watch as the steam floats gently toward the sky.

Why is this so important? The truth of the matter is that you only get one chance. You can't make that same mistake with the same person ever again. There is always someone willing to step in and work as hard or harder to ensure that it doesn't happen again. Mistakes usually come either from the stress and chaos of juggling too many things or from simply regarding something as less important at the time. Whatever new project you've taken on, you've got to give all your responsibilities equal time. What you discount and push aside right now as a low priority may prove to be more valuable down the line.

Now back to the big question. Does it matter if you were right? The producer *thought* he told me, but the truth was he never called or e-mailed me, and I never got the message. Does it matter if he knows that it was his fault and not mine? Here's the answer to that: NO. If the opportunity ever presents itself, it's good later on to have a laugh about it. But the reality is: It wasn't important then, and it's not important now.

THE POWER OF LOOKING PEOPLE IN THE EYE

I had heard all the stories about Quincy Jones. I had read his autobiography. I knew quite a few people who had rubbed elbows with him. But then it happened. I met him. It was a big music industry event, but I was immediately struck by a remarkable spectacle: Although the room was buzzing with what seemed like thousands of people, Quincy had this remarkable ability to make you feel like you were the only person in the room.

As I stood back and observed and felt the energy surrounding him, I realized that the reason for his incredible success had only partially to do with his incredible musical talent. His other gift quite simply went right to the core and was the groundwork for everything else he was doing. It was clear that Quincy had a magical gift for making people want to be around him. Furthermore, everybody near him felt so at ease.

His magnetism really wasn't some mystery, like he held a magic wand or some fairy dust and could cast a spell on those around him. It started with something as simple as looking people right in the eye when talking to them. In doing so, he opened the connection and transmitted the fact that he cared.

I looked at him and I said to myself, "That could be me." I recognized something in me that was like him. I knew that I also had that kind of charisma naturally wired into me, if I cared enough to apply it. By watching Quincy Jones, I realized that when your manner is sincere, it forges a bond that makes people want to work for you and work hard for you. It makes them care about you, too.

In Quincy's case, you always get the heartfelt sense that he's genuinely happy to see you. Whether it's a writer, a photographer, a bellman, it doesn't matter. He has that ability to make everyone feel special. He did it to me the first time I met him. I remember every word he said to me: "The first time I saw you, you were conducting for Whitney Houston on a TV special. I said, 'Who's that guy up there?' It sounded great. It looked great. And I've been following you ever since."

I want to emphasize that he's not being phony or putting on an act. He's not trying to make the janitor or the limo driver feel like they're rock stars. He just lets each person know that they matter.

He seems to have a memory that doesn't stop. "How's

your family doing?" "How's your daughter Sophia?" "How are your kids?" "How's your mother doing; does she still have that back problem?" How did Quincy Jones remember that the gardener's mother had surgery?

Quincy Jones has performed for presidents, kings, and queens and has produced some of the biggest-selling albums of all time, but he is still always gracious and respectful. As I said earlier, I saw him as a mirror of who I hoped to be— someone who is caring and compassionate about people. It's not lip service. People can feel his authenticity on an energetic level. What's more, it doesn't stop with just words but is also expressed in his actions. If he sees a need, he fills it. He goes right to it—without hesitation. He doesn't think, "Is this going to make me look good or create some media buzz?"

A caring attitude toward the people you work with can turn out to be the most important attribute beyond your talent in achieving success. It doesn't show up on your résumé, but I am certain that a few of the accomplishments you listed on there would not have happened without this quality.

So how does this translate to your results? If you show this quality to the people you work with, it gives them more confidence to be who they are around you. It allows them to take important risks and chances, and it shows them it's OK to make mistakes.

Taking it one step further, when you show people you care and make them feel comfortable around you, you also let them know that you expect more from them. When you give people boundaries, they will only go to that point.

When you remove the barriers and give them encouragement, you open up infinite possibilities. Your support might just be the very thing that gives them that edge, that record-breaking time for the sprinter or that song performance where the singer never sounded better.

Of course, you have to have the talent to begin with. Truth be told, chances are that someone has already done the things you want to do, or will do them, or maybe is doing them right this second. So what separates you from the rest? Desire? Discipline? Patience? Having that fire inside? You have to have all of these elements working for you in combination. If you have the desire and the motivation, but not the talent, it won't amount to anything. If you have talent but no discipline or patience, then you're not going to follow through. If you happen to succeed despite missing one of these fundamental attributes, let me give you this advice: Enjoy it for the moment, because your time in the spotlight will be short-lived.

There are times I see Quincy a lot and other periods when I hardly see him at all. Since early on in my career, he's been a mentor by his example, and he still is.

The Natural Act of Hitting the Wall
on American Idol

Within a few days of the start of the intense Idol *process, I can basically set my watch and wait for the alarms to go off. Everyone goes through it, some to more extreme degrees than others.*

I call this first step "hitting the wall," but you might think it would be better labeled a "misstep." In truth, it is really a vital adjustment we all have to make as we challenge ourselves to move our game to a higher level. Each and every one of the contestants puts themselves in a place where they have to hit up against a wall. Once there, the next test is whether they're willing to dig down deep to get past it. They will also need to accept and even embrace this step as a natural consequence of the process.

It is not a question of "if" or "when" the contestants will hit the wall. It happens quickly, and the sensation is like stepping onto a treadmill that's already going at high speed. Here's another apt description: Imagine one day you're shooting hoops at the neighborhood park, and the next day you're playing in the NBA Finals. No one can be prepared for that shock. So it's only a question of "which," because there is a good selection of walls to choose from. The wall can be as simple as an inability to memorize lyrics or melody.

Or it can be more complicated, an inability to focus or an inability to communicate clearly. One of the most terrible of all walls is an inability to be yourself, when things get so intense that your own voice disappears, and all that is left is the stress talking. "That wasn't me . . . I know better than that," the contestant will tell me as she's listening to the playback, disgusted at hearing herself trying to power through a note that she would normally sing with finesse.

There are adjustments that the contestants will have to quickly make when they inevitably fall off the treadmill. There's intense pressure to get back on fast or risk being left behind.

Here are the most common examples of hitting the wall: Breakthrough number one: protecting the health of your voice. You think that just because you can sing, you can therefore sing at will at any time. Not anymore. It's when you're called on stage to sing in front of the camera and the little red light that indicates the recording mode goes on—that's when it counts! It's not your choice to tell the producer, "Let's start the cameras now, I'm ready to sing." No, when you see your name on the production schedule, whether it's ten A.M. or ten P.M., be ready.

"No problem," you say. But no one on the show has ever sung every day for fifteen weeks straight. On this reality alone, some people hit the wall and go splat and never get up. It's not only the physical wear and tear on your vocal chords from your actual singing. In addition, it boils down to a clear and simple question of being able to focus your energy with all the external pressures and stresses around you, compounded by your fears and anxieties. Then, all of a sudden, after singing every day for a few weeks, you wonder why you have laryngitis.

Coming down with a sore throat is a breakthrough by itself. It usually goes along with having that beginner's attitude of "I have arrived. Here I am. Therefore, I don't need to practice. I can stay up all night laughing with my friends, talking on the phone." I give them two bits of advice: Number one: Text message. Number two: E-mail. I say to them, "It will do you a big service if you learn how to let your fingers do the talking and not your voice. This is your muscle. This is your money. The less you talk, the better. And while you're at it, watch your health, exercise, and eat well. But speak softly. Don't yell and scream. Once you win, you can yell for an hour."

Breakthrough number two: Getting serious. You may have to adjust your ideas about your life and the things that are happening around you. There is so much distraction. You're doing interviews, shooting videos, going shopping for wardrobe, going to rehearsals, and then there's the competition. The stress is unlike anything you've ever experienced. As I said above, fifteen intense weeks of singing every day is just the starting point. Your life will be busier and more complicated, and the stress level will be in direct proportion to your inability to manage things properly. You have to learn to embrace the people who are there to help you. So you might have to let go of your control of things like your makeup, your wardrobe, planning your schedule. You need to get serious about planning your personal time to make sure you get enough sleep.

When a contestant who is doing very well suddenly falls flat, it is usually due to a lack of planning and preparation. They didn't take things seriously enough. They underestimated what the song would require them to do. They missed a lyric or a note because they were up the night before.

Welcome to performance anxiety like they've never known. But dealing with a mistake may be one of the most pivotal moments of their life, a lesson best learned as early in the competition as possible. My advice to them is simple: Don't freak out.

Stay present in the moment. Remember to breathe. Get yourself back on track. To err is human, and the audience will be forgiving up to a certain point.

Afterward, you'll have time to reflect on what went wrong and take preventative measures so it won't happen again. Acknowledge what went wrong. Fix it. And leave any trauma associated with it behind you. That mistake has now moved on to become an important part of your preparation.

PART THREE

On the Way Up

THERE IS NO SUCH THING
AS GOOD LUCK

If I hadn't been . . . I could have if only . . . What if? . . .

We can all look back on our lives and try to find all sorts of explanations for how we got where we are. Cause and effect . . . karma . . . being in the right place at the right time . . . or the wrong place at the wrong time . . . a chance encounter . . . divine intervention . . . being in the flow . . . connecting the dots.

My theory is that few things are simply chance happenings. We are usually exactly where we are meant to be.

I got a call one morning from the great Grammy-winning singer James Ingram. He was doing an event that evening for a community-based organization in Los Angeles called the Brotherhood Crusade.

"Hey, I know it's last minute. But can you get a few guys together and come and play?" "Not a problem, I'll be there," I told him. Later that evening, we set up, rehearsed, did a sound check, and went to a backstage dressing room to wait until it was our turn. At the same time, a little girl was finishing singing "The Greatest Love of All." When she found out that I worked with Whitney Houston, she nearly lost her mind. She was so excited. She wanted to meet me. She had to meet me. So she came back into the dressing room where I was sitting with the whole band. Twelve years old, she couldn't sit still. "I can't believe it!" A few seconds later, she settled down. We said hello, and she started to talk.

"Did you hear me? Did you hear me singing, did you hear me?"

"No, I didn't get a chance to. I was back here. Did you have a good time?"

"Yeah, I think they liked me."

Before we had to cut it short to go onstage, I exchanged numbers with her mom and dad. For the next year, they called me periodically. "Do you think we can meet Whitney? We're trying to get things going. We're trying to get a record deal. Do you have any suggestions? Any names we can contact?"

A couple of years later, I went out on tour with Whitney, and we stopped in L.A. for a performance. I got a message from that little girl, who by now was turning fourteen.

She was sitting in the audience, in the nosebleed section of the Great Western Forum, former home of the Los Angeles Lakers. Her question, Was there any way that I could get her a better seat?

I was able to get her seats down closer to the stage and backstage passes. This would be as good a chance as any for them to finally meet. But after the concert, Whitney was right out the door, in the car, and gone. The poor girl felt deflated, dejected, and defeated.

This scenario went on for two more years, until finally, one day, Whitney was hosting the Nickelodeon Kids' Choice Awards. This same girl, now sixteen, was acting on a television series. I told her that Whitney was coming in for a rehearsal, and it was all set up. The girl was there. Whitney was there. She moved forward to meet Whitney, and a second later, the girl bolted out the door screaming, "I can't believe it, uh, oh my God!!!" But she soon gathered herself and came back into the building.

That little girl was Brandy Norwood. She had finally met Whitney. As time went on, their relationship grew to be one of great mutual respect. Brandy ended up playing her idol's daughter in *Cinderella*, a film Whitney's production company produced for television.

Needless to say, that's perseverance. She really wanted to meet Whitney. She idolized her. She wanted to be in her presence. She loved everything about Whitney—how she approached a song, how she produced her own movies. "She even looks like me," said Brandy.

As I said at the start, there are few things that are chance happenings. I'm a product of the fact that I grew up in Louisiana, went to school in L.A., and met a string of people who introduced me to Gladys Knight, Al Jarreau, and so many others.

It's what we do at these key times that dictate where we will go. What usually messes things up is that when we have our shot, we find uncanny ways to throw ourselves off the mark. Our antics can so easily kick us off the playing field and exile us far from the stream of opportunity.

Your talent was something that was given to you when you were born. Now, how do you take something that is so simple and so easy, like breathing, to its highest potential? I have no doubt that if Brandy hadn't met Whitney Houston, she still would have found great success. It had nothing to do with meeting Whitney or me. She stayed the course. She didn't need good luck.

SEDUCED BY A PARROT

I was about eighteen and still on the outside of the music business looking in. My friend's cousin, Bruce Talamon, was a photographer who was hired by a lot of the big record companies. Through his work, he became friends with Fred White, the drummer for the mega-group Earth, Wind & Fire, which was founded by his older brother Maurice White. Fred lived in an apartment in Hollywood and invited us to stop by.

On the way there, I was beside myself. Imagine getting to meet the drummer of Earth, Wind & Fire. As we were driving up, I saw that he lived in a really nice apartment building. We went up to his place and walked inside, and the first thing I noticed was that he had a parrot. Better than that, it was a talking parrot. I'm from Watts. I'd never seen a parrot before, let alone one that talks—though I had, of course, heard that such a thing existed.

The parrot was talking. Fred said something to the parrot. The parrot said something back. I was thinking, "Life is good. Fred wants for nothing. He's got a decked-out bachelor pad and everything."

Fred excused himself and went away for several minutes to a bedroom in the back. When he came back, his head was down. He looked depressed.

Now my mind was saying, "This guy should be on top of the world. He's in Earth, Wind & Fire. They tour the world. His drum set spins in the air while he's playing. How crazy is that? What does he have to be down about?"

Then he started talking. "I know I told you guys to stop over earlier, but me and my girlfriend are going through some changes. We're breaking up for now." So we said good-bye. I left there thinking, "Hmm, so even he has problems with girls." It's so easy to get seduced by the fantasy, whether you're stuck on the outside or have managed to wedge your foot in the doorway to fame and fortune. Okay, I admit that today in the age of cell-phone cameras and streaming video, it's harder to be as naive as I was back then. If a celebrity has a bad mental-health lapse, or falls flat on their face on stage, the embarrassing photos or video will be getting millions of hits on the Internet before the end of the day.

There is no happily-ever-after once you make it. Life may be good, but there's no free pass. You'll get a whole new set of problems, like an entourage and relatives you've never heard of before who need a helping ($) hand. Of course, you'll still have a lot of your old problems, now just dressed up in a more expensive and fashionable disguise.

Females who become famous probably have it worse in our patriarchal society, I'm sorry to say. Tell me how a woman of great fame and fortune can meet a man who is interested in her and not the status she holds and all the goodies that go along with it. Or else she may face the opposite problem and meet men who are intimidated by her success. If she's dating a lot, she's looked at as loose, partying all the time. So what does someone like that do?

Fame and fortune don't necessarily make love any easier. As we often see, getting into a relationship with someone as successful as you are might turn out to be a big no-no, against all odds. If that other person is out there traveling as much as you are, you'll never see each other anyway.

The people who make it, whether in the glitz of show business or in the corner office at your own job, have the same problems and anxieties as everybody else. They're just like you and me. Still, it's the same situation Fred White showed me back when I was eighteen. True happiness is being able to communicate with others and have peace, love, and harmony in your household. And, of course, music.

THE BIRDS AND THE BEES

Now that we're on the subject of love, I hope I'm not going to disappoint you. Maybe you were expecting that I would tell all about the wild life of a musician. If so, you might want to ask for your money back. The artists that I played with were, for the most part, wholesome family acts, so the temptation was not there.

When I met Karen, the woman who would become my wife, I was playing weekends at a nightclub called the Speakeasy in Hollywood. Karen came into the club with her friend Gwen, who happened to be going out with the drummer. It is safe to say that at that moment Karen wasn't interested in me for the fame. It definitely wasn't for the fortune. I made $75 a weekend—$37.50 on Friday night and $37.50 on Saturday. My rent was $100 per month including utilities, so between what I made at the club and what I was able to pick up with other gigs during the week, I just had my overhead covered and could save a little.

Karen saw something in me other than platinum credit cards, "A" tables at chic restaurants, and nice cars. She saw how I embraced life to the fullest. I was twenty at the time. When I saw her that night in the club, I felt an immediate attraction. Trying not to be too obvious, I parked myself strategically outside the ladies' restroom after I had seen her go inside moments before and waited for my chance to talk to her. It worked, we started talking, and the conversation continued.

We ended up going out to breakfast and talking into the wee hours of the morning. We were engaged and married by the time we were twenty-five. The ingredients to a successful relationship are commitment, communication, and acceptance. If I need a reminder, all I have to do is think about an old client of mine. He was a very famous performer. "I lost everything," he told me, referring to his bank account, homes, and other holdings. He had been married six times. "The first wife caught me with a woman who would soon become my new wife." It went downhill from there. "I can't help myself," he said. "All the women are beautiful. They all want me." I said, "They desire you because you have money. You have power, the most superior aphrodisiac. Nothing personal and no offense intended, but if you didn't, why would they want you?"

Just when you think you've arrived and you have all this exciting stuff happening, you have to realize that it is the beginning of the end if you don't set some ground rules for yourself at the start.

Sex, drugs, and rock 'n' roll. No one says, "Rock 'n' roll, drugs, and sex." Sex goes first for good reason. Don't get me wrong. Sexual energy is a good energy. It's vitality, the essence of our beings. We wouldn't exist without it. It fuels the love of life and the love of self we need to have in order to love others.

You're projecting that energy when you present yourself to the world, or whenever you walk into the room. Even when you're watching a movie, reading a book, or listening to a song, there has to be love, passion, and sex in your veins. That's what keeps you moving forward. But the problem is that too many of us get stuck believing that sexual energy is the ultimate, when it is really just the starting point of our capacity for love and bliss.

The reality is that you will be considered sexually attractive if you have any level of success, whether you're standing on a stage with girls screaming for you, behind a desk, or on a factory floor. It's all right to be regarded as powerful and sexy. But as you look to develop your life and your career, you have to draw the line. You know it instinctively. But when temptation is there, we always seem to want to push the boundaries.

OK. Let's just say that one of your co-workers is attracted to you and you're working closely with her, late nights. Sorry, you still can't go there. "But what if she comes on to me?" you may be asking. Dream on, it is still verboten. You can't mix that relationship.

You have to set a firm but polite boundary. You must tell that person, "If we are going to have a relationship, then it's best that we don't work together." Otherwise, in most cases, it simply doesn't work. If the affair falls apart for any reason and you still have to work together, man, is it uncomfortable to say the least!

I was on a tour. The guy was a security guard and the girl was one of the background singers. We were on the road for a while. They started dating. We would always say, "It's either tubas or harps." When they're walking around in love, all you hear are the little cherubs plucking those strings. When things sour (which ultimately happened), it's "bwonk, bwonk, bwonk, bwonk." Welcome to hell.

If you look at music videos, video games, and reality TV shows, all they're selling is sex and the idealized nirvana of financial wealth. This illusion is often far from the truth. Lightly scratch the veneer, and you'll often find an abundance of dissatisfaction and misery. For those of you who are working nine to five in a routine existence, this sort of entertainment is an exciting escape. Regard it as just that, but not as a way to live or structure your life.

Is this the road you want and the baggage that goes with it? For every action, there's a reaction (including unplanned pregnancy and sexually transmitted disease). There's cause and effect. If you go down that road, you'll have to be prepared to pay the piper.

POLY-RHYTHMS

Some of the stories I tell in this book speak directly about the principle of letting go of the illusion that you can change another person. Instead, I say that your energy is better spent making yourself into a better person that others might want to emulate. If you're dealing with a friend or colleague, where boundaries and limits are more defined, it's fairly straightforward. If you don't like the way someone is acting, the option is always there to close the door and walk away. In an intimate and committed relationship, it's obviously not as easy to run away or ignore the things about that person you don't like.

As sure as the day is long, we all march to the beat of a different drummer. Everyone has a different rhythm. The most important thing that we need to understand is that you can't change another person. People will do what they do, say what they say, act the way that they act. You can only change how you feel about their actions and how it affects you. Our job is to find out how we can fit into another person's rhythm and let them be comfortable being who they are and not take things personally.

For a while as a young man, I would always ask myself, "Why does Karen do it that way?" That gave me the opportunity to work on and gather the principle of rhythm. I came to understand that my wife's rhythm is totally different from mine. I learned that I didn't have to change my rhythm to conform to hers. Instead, I just had to find a way for hers and mine to coexist.

For lack of a better word, let's call these *poly-rhythms*. I came to understand that there were things that were important to her. Whether they were important to me or not, I still had to acknowledge and give her due respect because they were important for her. As I've watched my son, Sean, grow up, I've had to accept that he has developed his own rhythm, too. "Do it my way or you're wrong" gets old quickly. I don't need to impose my will. Without that tension, you learn a much different and ultimately more satisfying way of communicating to help each other grow and keep the sparks flying in the right direction.

THE GREAT PRETENDER

It's two minutes before my client is about to perform live on *The Tonight Show*. She doesn't want to leave the dressing room. She has that horrible feeling that her clothing is a disaster. "How do I look in this skirt? Maybe I should have worn pants?" She begins to question that her hair doesn't look right, her makeup is bad—the list goes on.

"Please welcome my next guest," Jay Leno is saying as we're standing in the wings. My client is still terrified. She's stuck. For a second or two, I contemplate whether or not to push her bodily onto the stage. Instead, I look her dead in the eyes and say, "You look great! Have fun."

Could she have looked better? There are moments when we all could. Could she go backstage and change into twenty outfits and still feel the same way? Sure she could. But a gig is a gig. Short of going out there dressed up like a clown, it's going to be OK.

If it's any comfort, some of the most beautiful supermodels in the world go through the same thing. It's ironic how painfully insecure some of them are about their looks, all because some art director said their nose was bad or their teeth didn't look right for the job. I told you in the very beginning that the idea of giving people more than they expect is a good thought, but it can be much tougher to execute in reality. As you have probably already gathered from what you have read thus far, the vast majority of the enemies that you have to deal with come from within. What I'm describing to you now is one of the more insidious ones.

I see it in the hallways and dressing rooms at *American Idol*. I've seen it in many of the rising artists I've worked with and even in performers who've made it. I'm not immune either. An advanced form of it hits me from time to time. It's called self-doubt.

When you're starting out in the music business, all you

want is the opportunity to play. Then, once you start getting a little recognition, you have the sense that "Now I've arrived." That's usually when the psychological game begins. The mantra runs through your head, over and over again. "I'm really not supposed to be here."

To make matters worse, you're not only thinking it, you find yourself saying it to other people. Someone says to you, "You really sound great today." You answer, "I'm really not that good. They've made a mistake."

Self-doubt is a double-edged sword. Its destructive side can make you cross that fine line between persevering to make a go of it and giving it all up as another broken dream. On the positive side, it is there to keep us growing and to stop us from being complacent. It brings to mind what the civil rights leader Dorothy Height once said: "Even the flea has a purpose. It keeps the dog moving." We can't rest on our laurels or just go on autopilot, like I learned early on when I messed up on that important math test to qualify for UCLA. It keeps us honest and reminds us that there are no shortcuts. With every new job, we have to put in the time and the effort. We can't cheat the process.

Self-doubt is that feeling of being at base camp, looking up at Mount Everest high in the clouds and questioning how in the world you're ever going to make it to the top. No matter what the project is, there are so many variables, so many people involved, and so many elements that have to click. It's a wonder that anything ever gets done. I can hear myself saying, "There's no way this record is going to be done on time. . . . This film will not get finished. . . . This TV show is not going to go on air live." But somehow, some way, things always come together. Sometimes, the results are so incredible that I don't believe it.

Self-doubt is born out of the insecurity we feel when we are trying something new. Changing your life and moving up to the next level can be challenging. The process of personal growth, with all of its rewards, can be a thorny path. It can give you sleepless nights, making you wonder if you really have a safety net below to catch you if you fall.

I didn't want to be trapped waiting for the telephone to ring, for someone to call me for work. It required me to take a big risk. Without risk, there is definitely no gain. Giving up the security of the status quo to venture into the great unknown brings with it withdrawal symptoms, anxiety, and insecurity that can wake you up in a cold sweat in the middle of the night. "Am I doing a stupid thing making this big change? Is there really water in that pool I'm about to dive into?"

So what's the antidote for this? An important key is to know the difference between a calculated risk and a foolish choice. You can't just take a risk based on a whim. You have to know all the facts. Before going out on a limb, write out your plan. List the pros and cons. Visualize yourself in sharp detail in the new situation. You may not be completely cured of an occasional bout of self-doubt, but it won't sabotage you if you're mindful of it and keep it in check. Remember that anyone who is successful started out just like everybody else, a little kid with big dreams. Guaranteed, they all had a plan.

SEIZING THE MOMENT

You hold the microphone tightly in your hands. Millions of people are watching you perform live. The band begins to

71

play. You hear your cue. You take a deep breath. In the next few moments, you hope that you'll hit all the right notes, not too sharp and not too flat. You won't forget a lyric. You won't fall, lose a heel on your shoe, or have a wardrobe mishap. Your hair will stay in place. The list goes on.

Whether you're about to perform at the Oscars or simply giving a presentation at work, fear and anxiety are going to be there. It wouldn't be normal otherwise. Your heart rate and blood pressure will go up. The adrenaline will kick in. If you don't find a way to quiet yourself and relax in the moment, all bets are off. Things that are usually automatic, like breathing or having good pitch on a difficult note, may become impossible. You will get very uncomfortable and it will be hard to hide it. It's not just you. Think how the audience is going to feel watching you. They're not that different from the dog that can smell fear.

Some performers have good reason to be afraid if they're not ready and fully prepared. For that, I can't help them. There's no substitute for doing the work. But more often than not, a lack of readiness is not the problem. The fact that you were selected in the first place to stand on the stage or to speak at a meeting was because someone thought well enough of you to give you the shot. For the other root causes of fear and trembling, there are lots of things I can suggest.

The key is to find the trigger point and work on it until it is neutralized. If you're timid about a certain note and worried to death that when you hit it, it's going to be out of tune, too sharp, or too flat, the answer is simple. You have to practice it. It's like basketball players who get into a funk trying to make free throws. You have to get up to the line and keep practicing over and over again for hours and hours. With the note, sing it, hit it on the piano, sing it, hit it, sing it, hit it. Make sure you're getting it just right. Do this until you have confidence that when you go to perform it live, it will be automatic, like breathing.

Whether you're just starting out or you're experienced but challenging yourself to try something new, I don't think you're ever beyond needing to have the occasional conversation with yourself. Before an important gig, I think, "Are people going to like it?" This arrangement started off in my head. I thought it up. I presented it. Rehearsed it. Now the band is about to make it come alive. The singer will sing it. Will it be magic?

I take that moment and reflect on my journey. I think to myself how fortunate I am to have been given this opportunity, and I give gratitude and thanks for everything in my career that has led up to this point. But then I go back to making sure that I, too, am ready, focused, and prepared, like a pilot meticulously reviewing his checklist before takeoff.

I go over everything. It's no different than packing for a trip. I know I've forgotten something. The odds are that I did. There's always something that was overlooked, no matter how small. Hopefully it's not that important, like I've left all the sheet music at the hotel and we're going on stage in fifteen seconds. The effect is remarkably calming when you are certain that you've dotted your I's and crossed your T's and paid attention to the details.

When a contestant on *Idol* or a rising new artist hits the wall, I have a talk with them. It may sound like a cliché, but it works. I tell them that being here is not a destination. This is just a temporary stopping point. So in order to continue on that journey, you have to give up all anxiety about the audience, the stage, and everything around you. You don't want to be stuck in a mental ditch. You have to say, "I've prepared myself for this moment. Now it's time for me to use all the tools that I have. And enjoy it."

To overcome your fear, you have to go to a place where it's quiet and where there's a safe space for a moment of reflection. Leave the crowd. Leave the noise outside, the security guard, the hairstylist, and band members. Just for a moment. Quickly let it all flash before you: your existence . . . family . . . friends . . . school . . . practice . . . rehearsals—all that it took to get you to that point. Remember that out of everybody in your town or city, you are the one there. What are the odds of that? If you came from a big town, it's even more remarkable because there were so many people to pick from. So many others could have been chosen, and yet there you stand.

I believe that 90 percent of the fear factor I am describing is due to those internal programs that you carry in your mind when confronting any risky situation. The other 10 percent is specific to when you hit the stage and see the audience right in front of you. Some people have a huge phobia about standing in front of a crowd. It's not just artists. Think about it. There might be someone you know at your job or at your school who purposely comes in early just to avoid walking through the gauntlet of workstations.

I say to these performers, focus on one thing. Look toward the back of the room and find one thing to focus your attention on. If the song is an intimate song, then reflect that, like a character actor. Play the part. Think about that emotion. Imagine that the person the song is about is right in front of you and block everything else out.

The human brain can be such a dangerous thing if you are always overthinking what you do and say. I've worked with artists who were too focused on what the public thought. Every time they stepped on stage, their thought was, "What is the public going to feel?" On the other end of the spectrum, there are artists who deal with this fear by totally discounting the audience or virtually ignoring them. That's equally deadly. The public can pick up on it when you're not being sincere.

Sometimes, the very root of this fear is the fact that people have a hard time forgiving themselves for their mistakes, let alone forgiving others. We all want to be perfect but we all have shortcomings. It's not a bad thing to aspire to be the best in your field, but not to a point where this fear and anxiety about failing or not being the best takes over your life. It can drive you crazy and cause you to starve yourself to look skinny or spend a fortune on plastic surgery. You end up wasting time on superficial imperfections and spend too little time on your soul. Hold on tight and don't let go. Seize the moment.

UNLOAD YOUR MONSTERS

Why are *they* doing this to *me*? Is it because I'm younger? Because I don't know as much as they do? Is it my lack of experience? The color of my skin?

Early on in my career, if you pushed the right button, I would take offense and let my emotions take over: rejection, anger, blame, spitefulness, self-pity. Under the right circumstances, I might storm out of the room. If I got wind that a certain person had questioned my skills or ability, I would become incensed. I would shut down. Because of my insecurity, I would take it personally.

How much easier it was to point the finger of blame toward someone else if things didn't go the way I thought they should. It could cast a gloomy shadow around me.

"They're going to be sorry! They're going to be sorry they didn't call me!" What kind of thinking is that? Regrettably, I was acting the same way the majority of us react. I took rejection personally instead of thinking, "Maybe they just don't know my background—that I'm well versed in many genres of music."

Had I been thinking more clearly in situations like these, I would have picked up the phone and called the person. "Hey, I heard there's a project you're doing. I would really like to be considered. I have a strong affection for this kind of music. I would love the opportunity to demonstrate to you what I can do."

Later on, when things started going my way career-wise, the same problem would arise. There were people who wouldn't hire me because they assumed I was too busy and consequently wouldn't give their project the kind of attention it deserved. "We'll hire someone less known and cheaper," they would say. "The audience isn't that discerning. They won't know the difference between a great band and a good one."

It's very tempting to fly off the handle when someone upsets you or hurts your pride. "You have a job coming up, and that should be my job!" "Why don't you call me anymore?" Maybe you even slam the phone down on that person. All it takes is for it to get out that you were very rude. The news spreads. You learn quickly how small a town really is.

Again, the same solution could apply. Every relationship

is different, but you have to ask yourself if you're comfortable calling that person and having a positive conversation. Even if you don't get the job, it's great to clear the air. "Can I take you to lunch? Can I come by for a few minutes and have a word with you?" Face-to-face is always best. "I really enjoy working with you. I'd love to be considered for anything that you think I might be right for." In five minutes you can clear up what might otherwise take you five years to correct.

Many of us are stuck in a victor-versus-victim mentality. The way out is to realize that you are already victorious. Going into any new situation, everyone starts with a clean slate. People have no reason to think of you as anything other than great unless you prove them wrong.

The good news is that you don't have to work as hard as you think to be accepted. Of course, we continuously have to work hard at sharpening our tools and our craft. But if you walk in with a defeatist attitude, it's like flushing all of your hard work down the toilet. Think of what you could do with all the wasted energy you spend trying to get people to like and love you. Or worse yet, the more toxic version: putting others down so you can feel better about yourself. Instead, relax and just let people get a chance to know you. What a tremendous relief it was to learn that my biggest problem was *me*. I realized that it was my mentality that was at fault. When I fixed that, things got better almost immediately.

When we are not willing to point that same finger of blame lovingly toward ourselves, we become locked in a seemingly endless, repeating cycle of problems. Think of it as watching the same movie over and over again, dozens or hundreds of times—the same story, only changing out the actors and scenery.

Letting our self-destructive habits and behaviors run the show makes it seem like we're always being followed by a dark, rainy cloud. Everywhere else there can be bright sunshine, but around us, it's thunder and lightning all the time. For some reason, we can't seem to get it right, no matter what we do. We pick the wrong school. We hook up with a totally wrong boyfriend or girlfriend. If we make an investment, it tanks. Every job we get never seems to last long before it implodes. And so on.

Chances are good that there is someone matching this description in your family or among your friends. If that person happens to be you, then I hope there's something on these pages that will wake you up and help you get on the right track. Otherwise, the downward momentum will continue to thwart your potential, and you will feel trapped and powerless. Instead, try being honest and courageous. Deal head-on with your issues, and if necessary, get professional help. Otherwise, don't expect the sky to clear anytime soon.

There are so many variables that influence us, from the mental to the physical, the spiritual to the emotional, the genetically predetermined to the situational. How can it be that although Cain and Abel grew up in the same household, their fates went in such opposite directions? It's like watching a horror movie and screaming at the character on the screen, "Don't go in there!" And of course the person goes right into where sure catastrophe is waiting for him. To stretch the metaphor a bit more, in most situations in life, there are at least three doors. Why do some people always seem to have a perfect record of picking the worst one?

When you're a young person growing up, it takes time to figure things out. The same applies to older people who want

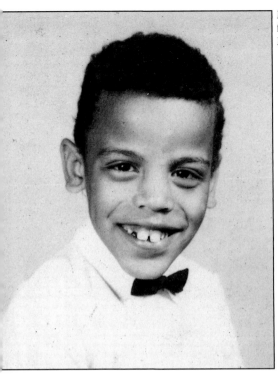

My second-grade school photo from Little Flower Academy in Monroe. *Courtesy of the author*

Our family home in Monroe, Louisiana, where I lived from birth until 1968. *Courtesy of the author*

The family celebrates the Fourth of July after arriving in California in 1968. Left to right: John L. Blevins, Jr. (brother), Helen Blevins (mother), Daniel Minor (uncle), Dixie Minor (aunt), Kathy Minor (sister), Cheryl Blevins (sister), Donia Minor (grandmother). Seated in front, left to right: Victor Minor (brother) and me in the middle. *Courtesy of the author*

My uncle Frank's army picture that was taken shortly before leaving for duty in Vietnam, 1971. *Courtesy of the author*

My musical journey begins with my first bass at the age of fourteen. *Courtesy of the author*

My band Potential. We had that cool funky look of a '70s band. Left to right: Donald Duvall (sax), John Davis (guitar—partially hidden behind Donald), Andre Greer (trumpet), Barbara Manning (lead vocal), Xavier Marshall (drums), Robert Smith (piano), and me with the big afro (bass).

Courtesy of the author

Me and my Mom at home in 1978.

Courtesy of the author

I took this picture at my first gig with Gladys Knight and the Pips. Gladys and her brother, Merald "Bubba" Knight (not pictured cousins William Guest and Edward Patten).

Courtesy of the author

In London for the first time on tour with Gladys Knight and the Pips.

Courtesy of the author

My wife, Karen, and I back from our honeymoon in 1984.
Courtesy of the author

October 1989, I became Whitney Houston's music director. The photo is our first day of rehearsal—a major turning point in my life.
Courtesy of the author

Hanging with Lou Rawls. He was one of the kindest men I'd ever met.
Courtesy of the author

Quincy giving me some invaluable advice.

Courtesy of the author

With Beyoncé Knowles at the Newman Scoring Stage, 20th Century Fox Film Studios, recording the National Anthem for the Super Bowl.

Courtesy of the author

Rehearsing with Christina Aguilera for her performance of "It's a Man's World" at the 2007 Grammy Awards, voted #3 of the Top 25 Grammy Moments.

© Rob Shanahan

Al Schmitt, Usher, and I put the final touches on the surround mix for Usher's "The Truth" tour DVD. *Courtesy of the author*

My wife, Karen, and Sting. He's one of our favorite artists of all time. *Courtesy of the author*

Sharing a moment with Herbie Hancock backstage at the Kodak Theater. *Courtesy of the author*

Hanging out with my son, Sean, and music legends Al Jarreau and Chaka Khan. *Courtesy of the author*

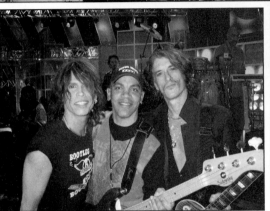

Working with Steven Tyler and Joe Perry at the Billboard Music Awards performing "Walk This Way" with Run DMC. *Courtesy of the author*

Conducting the orchestra for a tribute to Ray Charles that resulted in my first Emmy nomination. © *Ron Wolfson*

Onstage with my musical family. *Courtesy of the author*

With Bo Bice and Carrie Underwood at a rehearsal for the finals of *American Idol* 2005.

Courtesy of the author

My wife, Karen, our son, Sean, and I relaxin' at home in our backyard. © *Valerie Goodloe*

Working with B. B. King was a dream come true. He loves to tell stories.

Courtesy of the author

to continually evolve and learn. You can't just sit around and wait for things to happen. You have to act, try things on for size. And be mindful of one guiding principle: You not only have to *make* decisions, you have to *own* your decisions. How do you know if your problem is not being able to make and own your decisions? It's easy. The telltale sign is if you hear yourself saying something like, "I did this because my parents are paying for it." "My girlfriend (or wife) wanted me to do it." And last but not least, "My best friend did it and I figured if he could do it, so could I."

It takes time to realize that every decision you make is yours alone. Like my own example, you can't continue to shun personal responsibility by saying that it's somebody else's fault. First of all, it's wrong to refuse to take no accountability for yourself. But more important, when you have no stake in your decisions, you have no feeling of accomplishment. "I'm only here because my cousin got me the job, so I don't really deserve this job. I didn't do it myself. I didn't make it happen."

Having a healthy attitude about your actions and commitments in life will safeguard you from that vampire-like monster that can suck the lifeblood out of your potential. Not everything is going to go your way. Great innovation and inventions like the lightbulb happened only because their developers learned something useful from each *unsuccessful* attempt. But too many of us go into a major tailspin when our decisions result in failure. We use it as an excuse to stew in our misery and make everyone around us miserable in the process. We allow expectation from others and from ourselves to turn into a heavy investment of our ego and an unhealthy attachment to the outcome.

Let's say you wanted to be a professional baseball player, but you shattered your ankle and your aspirations are now over. "It doesn't matter what I do now. I'm not going to be happy since it was my dream to play in the majors my entire life." Obviously, that person has to get over the setback and realize that there are so many other jobs that he could do to stay in the sports field, such as manager, coach, broadcaster, or sports agent.

There's a reward for staying the course: great satisfaction and a fantastic feeling of completion. The same holds true even if you took a two-year course in electronics at a community college only to find that you don't like electronics. You'll find that your education was hardly a waste of time. Remember what I said about discovering the hidden benefit of those difficult math courses I had to take in college? I didn't go into a career in mathematics or business, but I never could have guessed how much those courses would help me in my music career.

Let me throw in one major caveat. You may think that a lot of what I've said in this book is all well and good and makes perfect sense. But it is all virtually useless if you've chosen to take the nearest exit off the highway by numbing yourself out. If you happen to have a problem with drugs, alcohol, gambling, or any other major addictions, it is an obvious sign that your monsters are running the show. Why do people use drugs and drink alcohol? If you ask the question of a troubled friend or family member, don't expect any deep philosophy. Their answers will be fairly basic and straightforward. "I like it." "I like the way it makes me feel." "I'm less inhibited." "I'm a man when I do it." "It helps erase the pain." Again, you can't jump back onto the game board of life and engage the opportunities waiting for you until you are willing to look at the truth of your situation.

So what is stopping you from waking up? What's your excuse? Does wisdom come with age only? Do you have to be a hundred years old to figure this thing out?

Again, I don't know if everyone is meant to take the journey toward success. I like to see everyone reach their full potential, but can they handle it? I think a lot of people don't achieve great success because they want it for the wrong reasons. Their motivation is completely wrong.

So if you need to clean up your act, here's what I recommend as a first step. The first thing that you have to do is STOP. Stop everything and pull back. Find a quiet space. Assess your situation. Take a look at where you are, what you're doing, and who you're spending your time with. Decide what things need to change. Is it where I live, who I'm hanging out with, what I'm doing for a living? Ask yourself, "How do I change?" Write it down. Lay it out. Trust me, the hardest part won't be the work itself. It will be leaving behind people who are holding you back. It may mean changing your circle of friends and cutting off unhealthy or codependent relationships—and family members are no exception.

You will be surprised at how things start to fall into place in a logical progression when you get clearer on the inside and begin to unburden yourself of illusion and delusion. With your eyes open, the negative patterns, thoughts, and influences that you once accepted as normal or chose to simply ignore will not be as welcome in your life anymore.

After you finish this book, I hope you'll be saying to yourself, "I can do the same things that he can."

I'm only doing what's humanly possible. So yes, anybody

can do what I'm doing and achieve their dreams. If this all sounds good, the last monster is the one that tests your will and your tenacity. Are you really willing to do what it takes? Everybody *wants the work* but not everyone *wants to do the work*. If they knew the kind of hours that one has to maintain, the kind of schedule and the intense concentrated focus that it really takes, a lot of people would beg off.

Each time you say good-bye to one of your monsters, you'll immediately notice a lightening of your load. Once you stop lugging around their dead weight, you'll be in much better shape for the journey ahead.

LION TAMING

One survival technique you'll need in the jungle sooner or later is the ability to deal with demanding and sometimes unreasonable people. The key is to master this as early as possible, since it helps to be increasingly better at it as you move higher and higher up the food chain.

For this reason, I was very happy to encounter Joe Mele. It is no accident that Joe has been a conductor, music director, and arranger for some of the best. He is really good. He is a no-nonsense kind of guy, but with a wonderfully dry sense of humor once you dig below the surface. He was conducting for Lou Rawls. I was playing bass, a newlywed and very happy to have the job, until one night . . .

We were on the bandstand playing before a packed house, the first night of a two-night stand. Joe was standing by the piano, and I was way on the other side. When we got to a cer-

tain part of the song, Joe suddenly started yelling and screaming something at me. I was playing and Lou's deep voice was
booming, so I couldn't really hear what Joe was saying. But it
was clear he was having a problem with me. There was nothing much I could do right in the middle of the show. I kept on
playing, and he kept on screaming in plain view of Lou, my
fellow musicians, and the whole audience. It was really embarrassing.

That night, I didn't want to go out with the guys to get
something to eat, even though I knew sulking in my room
would be only temporary relief. Being around all those people on the road, it's impossible to hide problems for long,
and unaddressed, they erupt sooner than later. Like the
"poly-rhythms" we discussed earlier, common sense told me
that my task with Joe was not to try to change him, but to fit
into his rhythm and let him be comfortable being who he
is—and most important, not to let the situation take me off
center emotionally. But this one was really difficult. It
pressed my buttons. Although I knew better, I did take it
personally.

So I sat in my hotel room, fuming and totally fed up with
Joe Mele. "How could he! Yelling and screaming at me like
I'm an idiot!" I made up my mind right then that I was going
to go and find Joe. I was going to quit. I didn't even want to
consult with my wife about it. I was just going to do it. So I
went down to the bar, and there was Joe with the guys.

I said to him, "Can I talk to you for a moment?" We went
off to the side. "Listen, I don't know what I did that caused
you to yell at me."

He said, "Well, when you get to this part, I want you to
play something different."

"So why didn't you tell me after the show?"

"By the end of the gig, I didn't remember," he said.

"So why don't you write it down and tell me later?"

"I don't have time to write it down," he said.

"I understand that. But if you can't talk to me and tell me what's wrong, then you have my resignation right now because I can't do it. I need this job, but I don't need it bad enough to accept this kind of treatment."

He said to me, "Listen, man, you're a young guy. You're playing your butt off. I apologize. I was yelling at you because I wanted you to hear me over all the music. So I cannot accept your resignation. If I find out what it is, I'll tell you."

I told him, "Look, I know the spot." Suddenly, we were getting to a harmonious place. "Why don't we take a look at rehearsal. I'll come over and show you what I'm playing at that point. If there's something you want me to play differently, then I'll do it."

It helped that I had been willing to walk away from the job if necessary. That action drew a line in the sand, a clear and resolute boundary. What Joe taught me is that you have to teach people how to treat you. They don't really know until you show them. They're used to treating you like the employee they dealt with before you. In Joe's case, the situation proved to be harmless. He didn't realize what he was doing. Who knows, maybe I was the first person who ever said to him, "Don't do this to me." He was just doing what came naturally, pointing and shouting, "Hey, don't do that! Stop that!"

The people I deal with can be demanding and high-strung, but most important, they're creative. Creative people are always pushing the envelope. Many times, they will be openly confrontational to test your mettle. Some will say it to your face: "Why do I need you?" They were successful before they met me, so it is reasonable for them to ask what special things I might bring to the table. So not only do you have to set your boundaries, you have to establish trust right from the start.

Of course, what I'm telling you applies to working not just with creative people in the entertainment business. There are similar dynamics at almost any workplace. People in positions of power and privilege want to stay there and will behave in harsh and sometimes inappropriate ways if that position is threatened.

Bottom line, you can't have any chinks in your armor when you walk into that room, because people like that can smell fear. They know right away if you're terrified out of your mind or if you really don't know what you're doing. They're used to pushing people around, demanding this, demanding that, being rude and otherwise acting less thoughtful than they should. Some treat it as a sport to see what it takes to intimidate you.

One last word of advice: What you say and what you do in these situations will not be forgotten. Be sure that you have what it takes to back up your claims. You get one chance to make a first impression. If you don't make good on your one shot, there will rarely be a second opportunity. In the unlikely event that your name comes up ten years down the line, someone will say, "Oh, I remember that guy. He didn't have his act together. He made promises. He didn't deliver." Ten years, twenty years later, it still follows you. My grandmother used to say, "You can get by, but you can't get away." You can fool a few people, but sooner or later it's going to catch up with you.

LION TAMING—PART TWO

What you've just read is all well and good, but let me make sure to give you this disclaimer. Some situations may be hazardous to your health, and the benefits of being in the fray are questionable at best. You have to know when to say enough is enough.

Sometimes, no matter how hard you work or how badly you want the relationship to be successful, it may be in your best interest to walk away. You can't fix every situation. The choice is more obvious when you're working with someone who is blatantly toxic and unrepentantly abusive, in denial about alcohol, drug, or mental health problems, or continuously out of control.

But before you come to the conclusion that this person is totally unreasonable and impossible to work with, give them one last benefit of the doubt. As I stated before, everyone has a rhythm, especially demanding artists. You have to find a way to work with them, not by changing their tempo or who they are, but by looking at how you can gel with their rhythm. If they're very high-strung, the first thing they may say to you is: "I don't like that arrangement! It's horrible! I hate it." Your knee-jerk reaction may be to immediately take offense. "That's my work of art. I created it." However, that's not a constructive way to defend your work, in my opinion. When dealing with a client who isn't in sync with your work, the onus is on you to make adjustments because they've hired you to do a job for them.

So the first rule is "Don't get personal with your product." Instead, ask for more information. "You don't like the arrangement? Tell me what you don't like and I'll fix it." The person may say, "I want more movement," or "The strings are going on for too long." And you might respond, "OK, I'll fix it."

Here's the golden rule. What I demand in all relationships (business and personal) is simple. I want someone to appreciate my contribution. I could be anywhere doing anything. I certainly don't have to be here. So, appreciate my contribution. Respect me as one human being to another. Regardless of whether we see eye to eye on everything, we need mutual appreciation and respect if we're going to move forward. If it's a job where there's payment involved, then pay me fairly. Combine that with respect and appreciation, and I'm happy. One without the other is a recipe for breakdown.

When I finally got into a position where I could leave a job that wasn't working for me, I did. I said, "You know, this is not for me." Even under these circumstances, I wasn't blaming the boss. It was just that I was unable to find the rhythm. It's always tempting to point the finger and say, "This person was not nice, I couldn't work with her. And that person also was mean, I couldn't work with him either." Instead, take responsibility. You put yourself into the situation and invited that energy into your life, after all. So it's on you. When you truly take responsibility for your negative choices, it can have the magical effect of helping you to see warning signs earlier and avoiding similar trouble the next time. And if you have the choice, why not leave things on a positive note?

When a job doesn't work out, don't take it personally, because it usually isn't personal. Sometimes difficult people are just who they are, and you just happen to be within target range. There are two types of people: those who make you feel warm and fuzzy, and then everybody else.

In the heat of the moment, there's no time to find out if there's some childhood trauma behind it. Instead, it's like being on a sports team. Are you both playing your positions? Are you carrying out your respective jobs? If the answer is no, then you need to stop what you're doing and regroup.

When you're working with a difficult person, in the end it's about trust. They have to feel that you genuinely care about them. When a problem arises, I'm not worried about the job they have, their status in the business—that is not what's important for me. I'm asking myself: What can I do to improve their performance? What things can I say to get them to focus on the job at hand?

Nothing's more gratifying than when you solve a problem on the spot and stop a potentially harmful situation from becoming destructive. I was once on tour with a client who was in turmoil. It was affecting the quality of his product and making life hell for everybody around him. It helped that I knew that he and his wife had just had a baby. He was taking a lot of flack at home because she was home alone with the baby and another young child. In her mind, he was just out there having fun.

My conversations with him were about how to channel that anxiety and stress into something that was usable. "When you're singing those lyrics about love, passion, and caring, put these feelings and images of your wife and children into your heart and emote that," I told him. "In that same way, try to figure out how to express to your wife how difficult it is for you not to be there when she needs you, and tell her how much you want to be with her, period."

In this case and many others, the most important thing I had to contribute had little to do with music. Sometimes, I have to be a friend. I'm always looking for ways to balance the polarity. Sometimes, there's only a hairbreadth between the positive and the negative, the salvageable and the hopeless.

If all of your efforts to create communication, trust, and respect fail, you can at least leave in good conscience knowing that you've tried your best. In most cases, the universe responds by presenting you with an even better opportunity, sooner rather than later.

Chasing Your Own Tail

*"Hey, I got the rehearsal tape and it's all wrong. It's all wrong!"
The contestant was livid. The band was watching, and you
could see they were all thinking to themselves, "Uh-oh, what's
Rickey going to do about this?" "Let me talk to you for a moment," I said. I pulled the person to the side so we could speak
in private. What I was going to say could be embarrassing if
heard within earshot of others.*

*"Listen, let me help you, because I'm sure no one has ever
told you this before. In order to get positive results, you've got to
put out positive energy. You may be right that this tape is all
wrong. But you're not going to get anywhere by talking to me or
anyone in that tone. There's a way to get people on your side
and to want to work with you. For example, you could say, 'The
arrangement is different than I thought it was going to be. Is
there anything we can do to change it? Here are my ideas.' Then
you take people off the defense. They'll instead go on the offense
and try to help you solve the problem. There is a way to say
there's a problem without coming off like a jerk. If you say 'it's
all wrong,' then it also implies that you know how to fix it. At
this point in your experience, it is unlikely that you will know
what to do or how to do it. Let's just talk with respect. Then I'm
willing to work hard for you, but without that, I can't." "I'm*

really sorry, Mr. Minor," he said. "Thank you for telling me. I promise you it won't happen again."

If I see someone I'm working with going down the wrong path, I try to catch them before they make a mistake. But sometimes, you have to let people go ahead and tank. It's in the category of "you can lead a horse to water." You remember the line I told them about how when your ego walks in, God walks out? I wish my job ended there. They may nod their heads in agreement when I tell them, but often they haven't really gotten it, and I'll probably have to sit them down and talk it through again. After that second talk, my job in this regard is truly finished. There's nothing more I can do. It's up to that person to recognize the problem and start dealing with it. But for some, it's a hopeless cause. They come in with their attitudes already deeply ingrained, and there's no way I can crack through that layer of concrete. I have to recognize where I should spend my time. There are some people I won't be able to help. They're too far gone.

But what's really going on here? Here's my take. They're reacting to the tremendous pressure. In an effort to show some control, they may be a little too assertive and make unwise decisions. I've had contestants tell me that everyone from their accountant to their soccer coach from the fourth grade is calling and weighing in with opinions. Do this. Do that. Don't do that. Smile more. Make sure you look at the camera.

It's fear. The contestants are not immune. We all have it, that big fear of failure. They get wound up. You see the little whirlwind they make by chasing their tails. There's too much going on for some people to focus and listen. They might have reacted differently to the situation outside of the competition. Had it been somewhere else, they might have made a better decision in the heat of the moment.

So it's my job to help them dial back in. Sometimes they hear me, sometimes they don't. All I can do is say to them, "I recommend you take a look at this. Here are your choices. Maybe don't do that. . . . Slow it down a little bit or maybe change the key." But ultimately, the decision is theirs.

This may be an obvious point, but let me emphasize it. I'm not there to give them protection from the judges, from the American public, their parents, or anyone else. I'm there to shield them from themselves so they don't do harm internally. I want them to feel that they can talk to me about anything. As long as there's respect, everything is on the table.

You must develop a healthy viewpoint about yourself and about the competition. If you are honest with yourself and give one hundred percent of what you have, then you can sleep at night. You have to be able to say to yourself, "OK, this is what the competition is. Simon, Randy, and Paula are going to say what they're going to say—about my singing, about how I look, about my whole approach. They may tell me I'm a copycat, that I have no originality, and so on. I have to hear all these things and process it."

It's bad enough if your teacher scolds you and it's worse yet if the principal calls your parents to school. But think about the enormous stress of hearing negative criticism with the whole world watching. You have to find a way to cope with it. Based on how you react and what you say, you may do irreparable damage to your career.

Quincy Jones has a saying from one of his lyrics: "You let 'em tell you what to say and what to write, your whole career will be over by tomorrow night." If you change every time they say your hair should be up instead of down, or you should wear a dress instead of pants, you're in trouble.

Fear and doubt creep in when you start believing everything that is being said about you, both the good and the bad. Especially the good. You get ahead of yourself. You think, "Everyone knows my name. Therefore, I am what everyone says I am."

That's the biggest mistake. The reality is that if you're fearful, you will not win the competition. If you are dealing with fear on a daily basis, it is going to eat you up. So you have to find a way to put it aside.

The competition process is about recognizing who you are, where you are, and what you want out of it. You have to be honest with yourself because it's not for everybody. Some of us are not gladiators who go for the jugular. For every spot available in professional sports or for every role being cast in theater, television, and the movies, there are a thousand talented, qualified people waiting in line. So many factors have to come into alignment beyond your talent and passion. If you carry a spirit of gratitude inside yourself, you will find victory even when things don't go exactly the way you wanted them to go. Savor the moment. Enjoy the ride.

PART FOUR

Making It

THE DEFLATED ROOSTER

When I first started out, I didn't know that much about the business of music. As a musician in a band, life was pretty straightforward. You played. You got paid.

I had a good job, playing bass for Whitney Houston. Things were going really great. Then, one day, I got the call to become her *music director*. This was huge, a giant leap forward in my career.

What caught me by complete surprise was that a bigger leap would be demanded of me from the inside. I guarantee that as you truly move into success mode in whatever you do, you will have to go through this internal shakeup, in one way or another. Consider it part of the journey.

The whole thing took less than an hour. But it is something that I look back on with fundamental gratitude. As usual, I see just how fortunate it was that the lesson happened then and there, the right message perfectly timed for the situation. Miraculously, I had the good sense back then to shut up and listen. Like a colorful prancing rooster, my ego walked in with me to the meeting I'm about to describe. But that rooster had the equally good sense to head for the exit and let some more intelligent common sense take over.

Back to the story: I negotiated what I thought was a really good salary, for me and for the band. As the last step in the process, I needed someone to do the final paperwork, so my accountant recommended a lawyer.

I went to the attorney and said to him, "Here's what the deal is." Before we even really started talking about the salary I'd negotiated, I went into full rooster mode and pumped up my chest. "*This* is what the band is making, and *this* is what *I'm* making, per week." I went through all the particulars, how I was getting a salary and a retainer, plus medical benefits. I told the attorney that all he needed to do was to put it all down in the contract. Simple enough, right?

The guy listened, but to my dismay, I had that sinking feeling that he wasn't so impressed. Hey, what was there not to like? These figures were big.

So I went on. And still, he didn't say anything. Finally, he opened his mouth. "There's only one problem."

My chest started to deflate. The rooster was getting nervous and restless. How could there be a problem? I had negotiated a humongous fee.

He went on. "I can do your deal. I'll put it in writing the way that you want. But you still have a problem."

How could that fee possibly be too low? Is he serious? He says I have a problem. Me? Come on, what does this lawyer know, anyway? My body language was now totally caved in and depressed.

"Let me tell you what your problem is. Your problem is that you see yourself as *a bass player*. You don't see yourself as a corporation. You should view yourself as a corporation with various divisions like Coca-Cola. So you've made a deal, an all-in deal, as the bass player and the music director." He paused with a deep breath and came to the point.

"Let me list some of the other things you will be doing. Babysitter. Therapist. Friend. Fixer. You'll get calls all through the night anytime there's a problem. When everything goes right, everybody will take the credit. When anything goes wrong, you'll get all the blame. For all of that, this is the amount you chose."

He wasn't done yet. It was getting worse.

"Now, let's divide that and see how much this works out hourly because your hours will cease to be your own. So this is how you see yourself, and it's a problem that you're going to have to tend to. Don't get me wrong. This is a nice amount for someone your age. But how long are you going to be able to say that?"

"I'll write this deal up. But you need to go home and write down your plan. Where do you see yourself in three years? Five years? Ten years from now?"

He took a look at his watch, signaling that our talk was coming to an end. "Let me tell you why this is so important. You can't get there until you can actually see it. You've got to envision yourself there."

Before I left his office, I had realized the truth of what he said, once I snapped out of "rooster mode" and put my foolish pride aside. I did see myself as a bass player, albeit a bass player who happened to be the leader of the band—but no more than that. It made me ask myself a lot of questions. I've got good organizational skills. I've got good people skills. Why shouldn't I be the leader? Why shouldn't I produce the records?

Why couldn't I be the music director for a television show, since I was doing it already for concerts? I knew what was needed. Furthermore, why couldn't I open up my own office, if not my own studio? Why couldn't I call the shots? Why couldn't I decide which artists I wanted to work with?

Like a reptile that sheds its tight-fitting skin to grow, we need to periodically strip away the close-minded thinking that can stop us from moving forward. The attorney's words pushed me to a new level . . . and continue to push me today.

ROCK THE BOAT

Having the vision to see yourself living your dream is essential, but that's just the start. You've got a lot of work to do. Your dream will stay just that and never get off the ground if you don't follow up with planning and action. It took a wave of technological innovation unprecedented in human history to make good on President Kennedy's challenge in 1961 to "[land] a man on the moon and [return] him safely to the Earth" before the end of that decade. Only a month earlier, the best anyone had done was blasting a Russian named Yuri Gagarin into space on a spacecraft that looked no bigger than a trash can. It's one thing to have a great idea, but how do you implement it?

Today, we live in an age of instant gratification. We want it fast. We want it super-sized. We want it now. The saying "patience is a virtue" did not come out of thin air. The same can be said for that other unpopular truth: "No pain, no gain." Regrettably, there's no such thing as an overnight success. You've heard some of what I had to go through on the way up. But it was a breeze compared to the dues the legendary

Berry Gordy, Jr. had to pay on his way to revolutionizing the sound of American popular music in the 1960s by starting a company called Motown Records.

Motown, along with the British Invasion of the Beatles and Rolling Stones and the California sound of the Beach Boys, tops the list when we look at the enduring musical legacy of that immensely creative era.

I think about the many odd jobs Gordy took to keep things going while Motown was in its embryonic state. He worked in a car factory, was a painter and construction worker, shined shoes, sold newspapers, and earned $150 a fight as a featherweight boxer. He took to writing songs and managing groups with what was left of the twenty-four hours in his day. It wasn't until he was in his mid- to late thirties that things started to come together. And still, it took another ten years of hard work before Motown was a profitable record company.

Piece by piece, Berry took his earnings and built a studio to record new artists while also working to set up a distribution network to get their records out. He created a dance studio and a grooming school, so the groups would have both the right look and all the right moves. He had to get the artists out on the road, so he came up with something called the Motown Revue and converted an old school bus into a tour bus. Each one of these puzzle pieces was instrumental. There he was, still not turning a profit and totally unaware that he was becoming a cultural icon (and that he would soon own the largest independent record company in the business). Who would have thought that Hitsville, the ramshackle house where he lived and worked, would later become a museum and be designated a historical site?

Were there other people in the business that could have done what Berry did? Anything is possible. I would have to say that there were a few who were talented enough and qualified. But few of them had all the other essential ingredients required: the vision, the enormous tenacity and drive, and the willingness to sacrifice and stick with it to completion.

Once you have your act together, then you can go out into the world from a position of strength. You will need it. In the entertainment business especially, people will see you as they see you, and you can't waste time worrying about it. I wonder how many people told Berry Gordy to forget about it, that he was crazy, that good enough was good enough, or that he was simply wasting his time.

There's also the "survival of the fittest" law at play, keeping you back in your place. As we talked about earlier, there's only so much room at the head of the pack. If you're an actor, you're an actor. For you to suddenly step into being a film producer or director, it means you're probably pushing another producer or director out of a job. You're not encouraged to grow. They don't want the competition. No matter what your profession is, the truth remains the same: You're encouraged to always remain the worker and not the boss. "Please don't rock the boat."

I'm sure we've all faced resistance from others when we've tried to move to the next level. Here's the main point: Things will start to shift as soon as we realize that *it isn't up to them—and it's never been up to them—to decide what's best for us*. Once we figure that part out, it frees us from having to contend with other people's judgments, whether someone liked or didn't like what we were doing. We must come to the realization that if we continue to work hard and focus, opportunities will find their way to us.

It may sound strange to some, but we don't feel pressure to "go and make things happen." By that I mean that what I manifest in my life never feels like trying to force a square peg into a round hole. Instead, it feels like a natural consequence of simply staying true to my vision and the process. I have to get ready and be prepared for what's coming next . . . because I know it's coming.

Envision yourself doing what you want to be doing and make sure you're actively pursuing the opportunities that will allow you to get there. It's no secret. As I've said before, if you want to be a mountain climber, you've got to go to the mountain; a surfer, you go to the ocean. You're not going to learn to climb mountains by staying on flat land. In addition to studying and acquiring all the prerequisite fundamentals, you also have to be around people who are doing what you want to do. That experience is worth a thousand words in your textbook. So learn your craft and study first. Then go out and put it into action.

Looking back on it all, I can remember the point when everything crystallized for me. It was 1977, and I was a senior in high school. My best friend in high school gave me a free ticket for an Al Jarreau concert for my seventeenth birthday. It feels like it was almost yesterday. I'm sitting there in my seat. I see it clear as a bell. It isn't "maybe one day." It feels like it's written in stone in my spirit. Silently to myself, I pointed to the stage where Al Jarreau and his band were standing and made a decision. "That's where I'm going to be."

CAN'T GET WHAT YOU WANT? MAYBE YOU'RE NOT READY FOR IT

Several years ago, I was working with Aaron Neville. He told me a remarkable story that dated back to the start of his very successful career as a solo artist and member of New Orleans' legendary Neville Brothers band. In 1966, when he was a young man, he had a huge hit song called "Tell It Like It Is." It was number two on the *Billboard* Top 100. The title of the song speaks volumes for what unfolded for him.

Aaron spoke with the kind of tone that left no doubt that he wasn't joking. "I'm so grateful to God that I didn't make it big when that first record came out."

I took a step back. Here was a young kid who had worked so hard to get a break. He finally had a record out. And he had a hit song. He had hit the jackpot. But one hit record doesn't make a career.

"If I had made it, I wouldn't be here today."

He told me that he was doing a lot of drugs at that time in his life and had very little self-control. He was absolutely certain that if he had achieved all the money and the fame right then and there, it would have killed him.

While Aaron's story is dramatic, the same phenomenon unfolds in our daily lives in chasing what we desire, whether we're after a record deal, a dream job, or a relationship. If it's not coming to fruition in the present, chances are you're not ready for it. "Tell It Like It Is." Aaron heard the message loud and clear. If we always got everything we wanted when we wanted it, chances are we wouldn't have been able to handle it. The Rolling Stones sang it another way: "You can't always get what you want, but if you try sometimes, you just might find, you get what you need."

I do have faith that somewhere and somehow, the divine hand is there, manifesting things in my life that I can manage, both good and bad. For me, it is about creating within myself the bandwidth. I say it all the time that the ego is about Edging God Out. When that happens, you're cut off from your higher power. There is no elbow room for God, guardian angels, or any other loving spirit you might believe in to assist you.

I believe in God. I feel the presence of a higher force. I feel it coming through in the guiding voices of my grandmother, grandfather, and uncle, even though they are no longer physically present. All I know is that it works as a great source of strength for me, especially when I'm facing challenges or adversity.

Just like Aaron looked back on his misfortune in retrospect as an enormously positive thing, I think that obstacles and problems can arise as great opportunities. They point us in the right direction and identify where we are stuck. They help us grow and teach us what we need to look at more closely if we would only stop for a moment and observe. If you start getting chest pains, for example, you are asking for bigger problems if you ignore such obvious symptoms. Difficulties tend to repeat themselves and progressively ramp up in intensity when we constantly ignore them and refuse to investigate their root causes.

Of course, nothing can penetrate through if we are in complete denial or self-delusion. Here's one example I'll never forget. A man once came up to me at some event and got right up into my face. He was very angry. The conversation went like this:

"You stole my gig. You have my gig!"

"What are you talking about?"

"You're Whitney's music director. I went to church with Whitney. That was supposed to be my job."

There really was nothing that I could say to this man that could crack through his anger and belief. I could only think about what a negative toll this man's feelings of victimization must have taken on his life. Had I served as one of his excuses for not achieving his goals?

For me, it has always been helpful to think of life as flowing water. A stream always descends from higher to lower ground. That force of nature is really beyond my control. I just have to let it go. The only thing in my power is to remove the clogs—the rocks and other obstacles—and make it flow easier.

To take it one step further, we are the ones who block the flow of our lives by casting anger, hatred, jealousy, and envy where they can obstruct everything. I don't know the formula for the exact cure for this sort of negative thinking. There are so many variables and factors both obvious and very hidden in our individual psyches that we each have to discover in our own time. However, I do have a rough sense of what the solution looks like.

It starts by committing yourself to finding and staying true to your internal flame. I promise you, we all have it. It's just that in some of us, the pilot light has been blown out. We all have to find that child inside that is yearning to explore, to try different things. It's that kind of spirit that drove people like Joni Mitchell, Miles Davis, and Tony Bennett to step out of their music, pick up paint brushes, and distinguish themselves as visual artists.

We have a lot of inner creativity, and tapping into it is

about getting in touch with that person inside ourselves who we love so much. This prerequisite is not negotiable. We have to *love ourselves.*

Finding that flame is the first step in getting out of our own way, like removing those rocks from the river. Finding the passion that drives you will lead you toward becoming freer from the shackles of self-doubt, fear, loathing, and depression. It also helps to remind ourselves that this life that we live is precious and fleeting.

Each moment of each day is to be celebrated. If we experience joy in one another, our jobs, and our friends, we'll find a celebratory existence in which we appreciate the trees, the rain, and the wind. When we have that spirit, we allow ourselves to flow. Positive things start to happen. It's contagious.

As long as you are still alive, it's impossible to find complete escape from daily problems and negativity. But fueling that spirit of creativity gives you a huge buffer. When you're in the light of that flame, you won't let problems dishearten or sidetrack you as much. Don't forget to laugh a lot until your face hurts. Enjoy the moment. This time, this moment, these circumstances, and these opportunities will never come again. Don't beat yourself up about every detail. Listen. Love. Learn. Elevate your game.

KEEPING YOUR WORD AND YOUR INTEGRITY

I got a call from a client. The person was in a total panic. "I need you," he said. The client was producing a big film, and working on it would have been a nice move up the ladder career-wise for me. The star of the film was going to sing for the first time. They wanted somebody who could work with a novice, a basic nonsinger. I met with the director and the producer and finally with the star. But in the end, the job went to somebody else.

A few weeks later, I received a phone call from the same client.

"Listen, can you do the film?" he asked (or more accurately, *begged*).

"Can I do the film? You told me a month ago that you were going with someone else."

"Well, we're having problems with this person. I've talked to the actor. We really think you're the right person. Can you do it?"

"I'd love to, but I'm booked for the next three months."

He backed off and said OK. A day later, he called again.

"Listen, this thing is really going south on us. Can we buy you out of that other obligation?"

I said, "I wish I could even entertain that thought. I really wanted to do this film. But I can tell you that I have never, and will never, break my word. I wouldn't do it to you if a better deal came along than your job. So my word is my word. I've made a commitment to this other project. After three months, if there's anything I can do, please don't hesitate to call me. But once I commit, I'm committed."

As it turned out, he didn't call me back for that or any other project. One door might have closed, but another one soon opened. It happened to be the chance to go out on tour with a rising young artist named Whitney Houston.

After all is said and done, all you have is your word. It

takes only a second to lose your integrity (and your reputation), and it can take a lifetime to get it back. You'll find out quickly what a ridiculously small world you live in if people start saying, "Oh, I'll never hire Rickey Minor because he screwed us." Your integrity means sticking with what you agreed to do when you signed the contract. You stay on budget. You don't pad your expenses. You have a clear understanding with your client from the start about what everything costs and what they're paying for. That way, at the end of the project, you'll feel great about it, and so will the person who is signing your check.

There's not only integrity toward others. You also have to treat yourself the same way. I got a call at home from a man I looked up to, a legend in the business. He said to me, "We don't have a big budget like the Grammys or like some of the other big shows get. So you have to give us a break on your price." What he was asking for was not a break, but a bargain.

The only reason this man was calling me at my home on a weekend was that I had already spoken to his line producer (who was in charge of the budget) and, after that, his executive producer. I had turned the job down to both of them.

"I'm honored that you've called me," I told him. "I'm thankful for the opportunity. But I can't make myself uncomfortable so that you can be comfortable. So it has to be a situation where we're both comfortable, or it's not going to work."

The sad truth is that you don't get paid what you're worth. You only get paid what you negotiate. So whatever that is, you have to be sure you're happy with it. You need to be totally comfortable with the deal you made. If not, your performance could suffer. There's nothing worse than signing an agreement and regretting every minute of it while you're doing the job. Money is not the only thing that will make people work hard. People respond to being treated fairly and with respect.

PLAYING THE TRUST CARD

Sometimes, the only difference between a major triumph and a devastating defeat is a decision you might make in a split second. It was 1991. I was thirty-two years old. I had been Whitney Houston's music director for about two years. She had accepted an offer to sing the national anthem at the Super Bowl.

We met up and started to brainstorm. We talked about other performances of the "Star-Spangled Banner" that she loved—one in particular was a version by Marvin Gaye at the NBA All-Star Game. He had sung with just a drum machine and keyboard. The song is written as a waltz—one-two-three, one-two-three. Marvin performed it in 4/4 time, and that's what Whitney wanted to do as well.

So, if you can imagine, it would go something like this: "Oh, say can you see (two, three), by the dawn's early light (two, three)." It gave her an extra beat every bar to take her time to be with the phrase. Changing the timing was the first thing that we did. I brought in Grammy Award–winning arranger John Clayton, Jr., who comes from a jazz and classical background, and I told him that I also wanted to add some gospel chords because that was Whitney's background—she had a soulful voice. So we had this crazy quilt of a classical orchestration with jazz and gospel influences, set to 4/4 time.

I took this arrangement down to Tampa and set up the session with the symphony orchestra there. They were in rehearsal for an evening performance with Academy Award conductor and composer Bill Conti. They had only given me their lunch hour to record the entire arrangement.

For a major event like the Super Bowl, you have to prerecord for safety. You just never know what might happen. The singer can get laryngitis or a cold, or any number of things can happen where he or she can't sing. But more important, there's the matter of the sound delay over the stadium audio system.

On the day of the event, each singer has the right to say, "I want to sing it live," or "I want to lip-sync to the track I've already recorded." My advice in these situations is always that you've worked hard to craft the perfect vocal, and you should stick with the recording. There's no way to prepare for the sound in a stadium full of eighty thousand people cheering and screaming.

You have the monitor speaker in front of you, but your microphone is picking up the roar of the crowd—and it's louder than your voice going into it. So all you're hearing in the monitors is crowd noise. Then you get the slap back. You sing, "Oh say." A few milliseconds later you hear "Oh say" back again. In the end, you lose your place because you don't know what the last note was, and when you started and ended it because of the reverberation in the stadium.

So, back to the orchestra. . . . They went through the arrangement and played it. The symphony conductor told me in no uncertain terms that the arrangement wouldn't work.

Not only that—the other bigwigs were around, and they, too, chimed in about how bad they thought it was. To be fair, keep in mind that Roseanne Barr had recently performed the national anthem in that infamous version at the San Diego Padres game where she was spitting and scratching her crotch. It didn't help that it was also right in the middle of the Gulf War. So it was a risky thing to change the national anthem.

They called me into a room and told me, "Listen, we don't like this arrangement. The orchestra conductor is telling us that it doesn't work harmonically. They say that you just don't write these notes together. It sounds so dissonant and strange." Then came the ultimatum. "We've heard it. We don't like it. What are you going to do about it?"

"There's a call for you from the other room," a production assistant interrupted at that moment. I went in, and it was John Houston on the phone, Whitney's father and manager. He told me, "We've worked hard for this. You have to be cooperative and work with these people. This is an important moment for Whitney." He went on to say that people were saying that I was being difficult because I was telling them how the song was supposed to sound and demanding that it had to be my way. He ended by saying, "You have to work with them."

At that moment I had to make a decision about whether to stay the course or go with what everyone had said. I thought deep, hard, and quickly! But there was no doubt in my mind. The arrangement was incredible.

I told Mr. Houston, "My interest is in Whitney. I want to do the best job that I know how. You've got to trust me."

It was the first time that it dawned on me that there comes a moment in your life when you have to pull out the "trust card." You've got to lay it out on the table. Bam! Here it is! "Trust me." You're telling someone, "If you pick up that card, you're giving me the authority to make decisions because you trust me."

"OK, little fellow," he said. "Just don't mess it up down there." I got off the phone and went back into the room. I took out that same card and said to the symphony, "This will work."

They said, "OK, we have a stock version that all the orchestras play. We want to record that as well. Then you can let us know which version you want to do—yours or the one that everybody knows and loves." So be it, I thought, but I stayed the course in my conviction and used the arrangement that I brought to Florida.

I took the tape and sent a copy to Whitney so she could listen to it in preparation for our recording session. When she arrived at the studio in Los Angeles, it was clear that she hadn't listened to it. I met her at the car.

She said, "I'm sorry I'm late." She was excited, in high spirits. "My agent thinks that I can get into acting. I just came from reading a script." It was an audition for *The Bodyguard* with Kevin Costner. "I think I did pretty good."

We walked into the studio. She said, "Play it for me." I had spent a lot of time on the arrangement. It was different and yet passionate. I played it. She listened. She sang it one time, and her vocals were quite simply amazing. I had her record one more time just in case, but what we ended up using was primarily the first take.

She came to the stadium on the day of the game. She decided to take my advice and lip-sync. There was a television commercial just prior to the national anthem. The executive

producer of the pregame show, Bob Best, had asked us to record a second song, "America the Beautiful," to be played on
the big screen in the stadium for the crowd during the commercial break. While the song played, they showed images of
American men and women in uniform, since the Gulf War
was still in progress. Whitney sang it in the style of Ray
Charles. By the time we came back from commercial and it
was time for the big performance, the crowd was completely
fired up.

You have to make a stand. At some point, everybody has
to make an informed and totally confident decision that can
change the course of their life. I could have lost my job and
my reputation. I had the orchestra in mutiny, not to mention
the network and Whitney's father.

Today, Whitney's Super Bowl performance is considered
by most to be the benchmark of all national anthems. The
orchestra, also present at the Super Bowl performing to the
track, saw the audience's reaction and was happy to be a part
of the performance. Since then, I've produced eight more
Super Bowl performances for an array of artists, including
Alicia Keys, Beyoncé, the Backstreet Boys, Barry Manilow,
Mary J. Blige, Earth, Wind & Fire, and Marc Anthony. It goes
back to my barbershop quartet singing days. You can't move
forward when you're only giving people the same thing all the
time. You've got to go outside the box. You have to think and
believe in your vision. It's not that you're that much better
than the guy before you, but you've got a little something extra to add to the pot.

Truth be told, I would not have been able to face the resistance and felt comfortable moving into something so different were it not for one thing—the confidence of Whitney

and her father. Whitney's response when she was told about the conflict was "Let Rickey do it." She trusted me with her career. By the way, I never had to use that "trust card" again with Whitney's father. I stored it away for future use, just in case.

EXPECT (AND EMBRACE) THE UNEXPECTED

I talk and talk about the importance of preparation. When you have done all the proper groundwork and planning, things will unfold just as you envisioned, right? Sorry. I wish that were the case. But that happens only in a perfect (and infinitely more boring) world.

Get used to the fact that everything you plan, even with the best intentions, won't go the way you expect. This doesn't mean don't plan. Instead, be bendable so you won't be breakable. When you're flexible, you have the capacity to handle the spontaneous things that can and will happen.

Everything I work on is time sensitive. Everything has a budget. Time and money set the boundaries. If the Super Bowl is going live on January 27, I back into it. Six weeks in front, I look at the calendar and map out realistic deadlines so all the puzzle pieces will fit into place. The first step is to meet with the artists and get a sense of what they're looking for in terms of tone and emotion.

Because it's such an iconic moment in front of an audience measured in hundreds of millions, the mood of the public also figures into the mix. Right after 9/11, people wanted big and passionate, so we had the hundred-piece Boston Pops Orchestra. The next year, there was a shift when the Dixie Chicks performed. It was decidedly more intimate, and the setup was small. But the effect worked just as well as if they had been a huge ensemble. They're great musicians, and they wanted to play their instruments, pure and simple.

Two years later, in 2005, Alicia Keys was set to sing "America the Beautiful" for the pregame program. Don Mischer, the executive producer, and I thought about what could make it special. Of course, an amazing talent like Alicia Keys with just a piano would make everybody happy. But then we had this idea about how to make it into a bigger event. Little did I know we were creating a little snowball that would start an avalanche.

We proposed to Alicia that she could do the song as a duet with Ray Charles. The only catch was that Ray had just passed away, but through technology we could create a wonderful tribute to him. The first step before taking it any further was to find out if there was any usable video and audio of him singing the song. I had recently done some work with his organization. His office called and said that they had just what I wanted. Not only that, the footage was already transferred into a state-of-the-art digital program that made it virtually turnkey, ready to go. It was a gift that fell into my lap.

I got to work and lifted out Ray's voice, surgically removing all the background music. Alicia would begin the song in a different key and tempo. The plan was that after she finished with "from sea to shining sea," she would turn skyward to the big screen and say, "C'mon, Ray." Before he starts to sing, he asks the audience to begin singing with him. Now it would turn into his version, and I produced Alicia's vocal to answer to him.

Again, in a perfect world, this was a slam-dunk. But then Don Mischer came up with another idea. The Super Bowl was being played in Tampa, near the school that Ray Charles attended, the Florida School for the Deaf and Blind. Why not have students from his alma mater serve as the chorus! The idea grew bigger and bigger. There would be 150 blind students who would sing. Added to that, another 150 deaf students would do the simultaneous translation into sign language.

This idea was not mine. I could have said, "We should keep the focus on Alicia and Ray." There were other reasons why I could have rightfully closed the door to that opportunity. Based on my carefully planned schedule, there was hardly time to go to the school and teach 300 kids, half of whom were blind and couldn't see me or read the lyrics. Then I'd have to design a way for the other half, who were deaf, to be cued to sign exactly in the tempo to a song they couldn't hear.

One other wrinkle was that we had the grand total of a 120-second commercial break to get the stage assembled on the field with 300 kids in place. It wasn't going to work to just tell them, "Go this way."

So all of these factors weren't in my original plan. I approached it with the attitude that anything is possible. It may take some extra thought. It may take extra manpower. But it is possible. If we entertain the fact that anything is possible, then it's just up to our creativity to figure out how to do it.

The important thing is you can't jump into the decision without thinking. You can't just do something because somebody made a suggestion. Nor should you reject something outright without giving it deeper consideration. Regarding this extravaganza, my first checkpoint was based on the practical impact it would have on my delivery date. More important, the final decision rested on whether it would raise the quality of the performance itself. You can judge the results for yourself by watching the whole performance on YouTube. Given what we all went through, it is remarkable how simple, effortless, and perfect the whole thing appears.

With everything that I do, I expect changes up to the very last second. And sometimes, the outcome goes well beyond original expectations—at times it's even historic. Somebody cancels. Pavarotti got sick the day of the Grammys. Coincidentally, Aretha Franklin had sung the same song he was scheduled to perform at a tribute to him a week earlier. She stepped in. In 2000, Josh Groban must have been grateful that Andrea Bocelli was ailing and couldn't rehearse "The Prayer" with Celine Dion. The producer got him to step in. That single act of singing during the rehearsal in front of a lot of the Grammy nominees paved his way to becoming a major international star.

Josh's story drives home the fact that you never know when opportunity is going to knock. Wonderful things can come out of something you thought was unimportant. If you're not open and ready for one opportunity, chances are good that you won't be ready for the next one, either. You can't control when an opportunity will come, but you can focus on improving your skills to be ready when one does arise. When I say ready, I don't mean that you have to be the best in the world. I mean ready based on your own ability and your own growth. It's back to my point about being on the journey and not at the destination. Maybe you've gone from a zero to an eight. And that may be exactly what they're looking for. You've made it that far. Keep your ears and eyes open. Take a step back and take a look and see.

Embrace the unexpected. It's coming.

Minor Adjustment

Tuesday, the day we go live with the performances on American Idol, *begins with a morning rehearsal. Each contestant is on stage to run through the song that they've been practicing all week.*

It gives us an opportunity to test everything—lights, camera, sound, video projection, and so on—to make sure all systems are go. Does the performer want a hand mike or a microphone stand? The end of the song might get some last-minute tweaking: "Why don't you pause a beat here?" Final decisions are made.

After all, somebody will be going home by the end of the night. There is one small consolation: Each of them knows that his or her performance doesn't have to be perfect for them to survive. They repeat in their minds over and over again: Just don't be the worst. Just don't be the worst.

The rehearsal can be a humorous sight when you've only seen the final product on TV. The smoke machine is puffing out a moody fog. The video backdrop adds another layer of texture while a young woman moves through a passionate love song. After her performance later that night, people around the country will be talking almost as much about her hair and how good she looked in her dress as they will about her singing. Before all the glitz and glamour, there's a dose of reality while looking at her right now.

A few weeks ago, she was waiting tables or working a sales job no different than millions of us. At rehearsal, she stands with the microphone in her hands, big curlers in her hair, a tank top and well-worn jeans. Squint and you could just as easily imagine her putting wet laundry in the dryer at the Laundromat. Yet, in a few short hours, she'll be live in the living rooms of more than thirty million people.

The evening before the live appearance that week, I called them all together for another talk—a refresher course, if you will—of that first lecture I gave them. Don't get me wrong. It is no accident these contestants are here. Their talent rose head and shoulders above the multitude. If I were in their shoes in this pressure cooker would I be acting any differently? Probably not. Who am I to cast the first stone?

I got their attention very quickly by the tone in my voice. With all the emotions running rampant, someone had to sit them down and be a voice of reason. This is a prime example of when I have to be the thermostat instead of the thermometer to bring the fever down. With the glare of the bright lights and all this attention, someone who cares about them needs to wake them up and help them understand that it's not all about them.

I found that they were not accepting their responsibility in this relationship. They were exercising the age-old science of finger-pointing. "It has to be someone else's fault. It's not me. There's a problem with the sound system. I couldn't hear myself. I didn't like the horn part and that's what made me mess up. The guitar was too loud. The drums weren't playing loud enough."

Is there any truth to it? Maybe. There's no such thing as perfect conditions for battle. The game is what it is. It's no different for you than for anybody else in your shoes. Who knew it

121

was going to be snowing in the middle of a championship game? When you go up to bat, you don't know which pitch you're going to get. You may get a slider, a sinker, a curveball, or a fastball. You know the conditions up front. So you have to laugh at fear. You have to look adversity right in the eye and say, "Look out, I'm coming after you!"

In the real world, even if the sound is perfect and the mix is perfect, does that guarantee that you'll have a perfect vocal? I don't think so. There are going to be things that will happen that are not helpful or conducive to what you want. So the challenge is to not make excuses. The mantra is simple. Just do the best you can.

In the same way that positive energy is highly contagious, being negative also spreads. Under stressful circumstances, when all of our buttons are pushed, each one of us has the ability to cross over to the dark side. You may find yourself complaining even when it's not in your nature because everybody else is doing it. Come to think of it, the refrigerator in my dressing room is supposed to be stocked with my favorite food. Who put all this garbage in here? See how easy it is?

I go on with my version of the coach's halftime speech in the locker room. "You have to decide where you are in this relationship. All I need from you is to carry your own weight. It's that simple. I don't need you to do anything for me. Take care of yourself. Work on your vocals. Work on your pitch. Work on being a better person, so when you leave this competition, you have a renewed spirit, a renewed mind that is all about improving yourself. You have to decide how you're going to be remembered."

The next morning, there's a different attitude, or so I think. The contestants are respectful, the essence of humility—kind and polite almost to a fault. Looking at their faces one by one, I know the chances are good that after this program I will never see them again. All I can hope is that they will walk away with something of value from our time together.

I realize then and there that what's making them so terrified is the next big breakthrough ahead of them. Someone is going to go home tomorrow. It's a harsh reality. By now, the novelty of being in the spotlight has begun to wear off. Within the course of a few weeks, they have gone from a place of total insecurity to another tenuous place of saying, "Yes, I am good." But then they start to hear those disturbing voices of doubt. Their minds go into overdrive and they begin to obsess about what's good.

I try to tell them that they will get more out of the opportunity if they stop, look, and listen. "You can't tell everybody how to do their job when you haven't figured out how to do your own."

But I also realize it's not only the fear and the anxiety. They're also dealing with the feeling of "I want this so bad!" "I'm willing to do anything I can. What can I do?" I repeat to them what I had said before. "You can't control everything. There are too many variables. Let's just say that you were fretting about the arrangement. You wanted more guitar. You didn't want the strings. But at the end of the day, you can get voted off for completely different reasons. Perhaps the people at home just didn't like what you were wearing or thought your hair looked funny. There are too many variables that will affect what happens in your life." They presume they can control what happens because they want to win so badly. And so would I! We all would try.

I don't have a magic potion. It's not within my power to

save the contestants from themselves. But it's comforting for me to think that one person heard what I had to say, and that it stopped them from imploding.

Back to the rehearsal, the woman with the hair curlers finishes her song for the second time. She feels giddy about her performance and walks over to joke with the staff sitting in the near-empty audience area. The next contestant is called to the stage over the loudspeaker and seconds later takes his place.

We start the first run-through of the song and two minutes later it is done. Only this time, we don't go right away into the retake. I put my bass down and walk toward him from my position on the stage. For five minutes, we talk. I go back to my position, and he does the song once more. He starts singing again and, to my disappointment, there is no change from his first performance. It is clear that my breath has been wasted. In these cases, I learned long ago that you have to shake it off. You can't beat yourself up over the ones you couldn't save. "If only I had stayed with him a little longer, things could have turned out different." Sorry. There's nothing that can be done if someone is so convinced that they have the answers and don't need help from me or anyone.

This young man had decided he was not going to sing what he had practiced. He had probably gone home the night before and made up different notes and different runs to add a little extra to what he thought was expected of him. He didn't consult with the vocal coaches. He just did it. The arrangement we played was the same. But what came out of his mouth was totally different from what he had rehearsed.

In his mind, he was trying to create excitement. "I'm going to showcase how I can really sing." He wanted to blow things wide open.

"You have worked very hard to get to this point," I had told him in between his performances. *"You have worked very hard on this song. Why change the game plan now?"*

I went on. *"You've got to connect to the song's lyrics. People have to believe what you're singing."* He didn't listen to me. As I said earlier, he did the song one more time exactly the same way he'd done it before. He went on the show that night and did the same thing.

Is the customer always right in this situation? The customer is only right when he's right! He's going to do it anyway. I knew right then and there that he was taking a big risk. He had been prepared, and he had thrown all of that away.

It wasn't long before he was off the show.

PART FIVE

Staying on Top

ONE HIT WONDERS—NO WONDER

I was the music director for a TV special. A young group walked onto the stage for their rehearsal. They were riding high. They had a huge record, the number-one song in the country. Oh boy, here we go again. It didn't take more than a few seconds before the racket started. They were being really loud and disrespectful to the audio technicians and the crew.

"I can't hear this!"

"Turn this thing up!"

"Where's my mike? Who's got my mike? My mike sounds horrible!"

I waited until the right time, the lunch break, and found them. I pulled them to the side and said, "I'm really excited for you. Your record is really doing well. That must feel great."

"Yeah, man, we can't believe it, *blah, blah, blah.*"

Before I go on any further with this story, let me stress one point up front. We're not talking about bad people. We're talking about good people not knowing any better and doing bad things.

I said to them, "I need to tell you that I'm very disappointed in your behavior."

"What? What do you mean? We didn't do anything."

"It's about those people you were talking to when you

were going on about the mikes and how things weren't right and this and that doesn't work.

"It's not the information—it's the presentation. It was the way you said it that needs to be changed. This is not acceptable. It's not acceptable here or anywhere. You won't be able to get away from these audio guys if you have any further success in this business. These are the same people who work on the Emmys, the Grammys, the Oscars. Do I need to go on? It's all the same people."

I told them that the one percent of all performing artists who make it, those who get the lion's share of the gigs, get to that place not only because they're extremely talented, but also because they know how to be appreciative. For example, country artist Travis Tritt may have two Grammys and a highway named after him in Georgia, but that doesn't stop him from being one of the most gracious people in the world. Once, when we were scheduled to rehearse with him before a TV special, he walked into the room early and heard the band rehearsing with another artist. When his turn came, he said, "Man, you and that band sure sound good. I can't wait to hear what you did with my song."

Elton John came onto the stage at rehearsal and sat down at the piano.

"Sorry it took so long to get back to you. What key did we end up in?" he asked.

"It's in E flat," I told him.

"Oh, that's way too high for me. Would it be a problem if we took it down a little?"

When you're so respectful, nothing's a problem. That leads right into the next point I made to these young men.

"I think when you go out there after lunch, you really need to apologize to the crew for your behavior. And they will be on your side. Remember, you need them more than they need you. Let me tell you something. If you find yourself out there hanging, like your mike is not working, they're not going to go that extra step to help you.

"This success you're having is short-lived. Anyone who's had it will tell you so. Neither you nor I know where we're going to be next year."

They did go out and apologize. They weren't bad young men, just new to the process. They needed somebody who cared to tell them about the process. The sound technicians can't. They have a show to put on. They're not in a place to intervene with the artist. Even if they could, they couldn't fix them all, and for that matter neither can I. But it sure doesn't hurt to try. Maybe I saw in them the potential that they had and the opportunity they were about to lose.

The artists you meet on the way up before the big number-one hit are really nice and sweet. But as their fame and fortune rise, they can get really ugly. Once they are on top, they look out and say, "The air is so nice up here." They soon inherit more family than they can count. They've even got an entourage. But when the money's gone and the spending ends, the party stops and your friends don't come around anymore. As the lights dim and the artists make their way back down to reality, they magically transform back into super-nice people.

People come up to me from time to time and say, "I remember what you told me when I first moved here. I've carried it with me ever since." It's great when someone thanks me for having some sort of positive impact on them. If anything,

I was just passing along what the elders told me when I was young and green.

It's a good reminder that you never know how your words and actions will impact people. One-hit wonders learn the hard way how fast the attention can disappear. So each job is as important as the next. You can't rest and say, "I got to the top of the charts, so now I'm done," because you're not. You don't want to become a "where are they now?" The fact is that if you're not putting in the time to work on your craft, you're just taking up space until your competition inevitably passes you by. This is why some of the world's greatest concert pianists, well into their seventies or eighties, still wake up and practice for two or three hours a day.

You constantly have to focus your energy on going above and beyond and doing the best job you can. You have to study, study, study. You can't know too much about anything.

In many ancient civilizations, elders would pass down wisdom and traditions as rites of passage to the youth. Now, advice is advice, so take it with a grain of salt, but listen because chances are good that there's something of worth if it's coming from someone who has lived longer and experienced more than you have. With the young group I called out at the rehearsal, or with anyone else I advise, the ball is always in the listener's court, and it's up to them to decide whether to be open to listening and learning or to discount the information.

To anyone who asks for my advice and chooses not to take it, I want to be clear that I'm not giving up on them. We have a finite time on this earth. Where we spend our time counts. I believe that everyone we meet is worth our time, although not everybody is *ready* for it.

Whether we're talking about me speaking to the young

band at the rehearsal, the elders who spoke to me at the musician's union, or the attorney who said I had made a bad deal, all of this advice was given with a pure intention to help. The message we all conveyed was the same: I want to talk to you, and I hope you're ready for this conversation.

If you're not, then perhaps there will be another time, or someone else will come along to have this conversation with you. However, if you're not ready to take action, then I don't want to give you the ball because you'll fumble it. Maybe at this moment, it's meant for someone else.

ALL THAT GLITTERS . . .

When things start to go well, it's so easy to get caught up in all the fantasies and material trappings of success, especially the most ridiculous of them all—taking yourself way too seriously.

I received a call from R & B singer and songwriter James Ingram. A meeting was called at his home. I was anxious to see his Grammy. I have to admit that when I entered his house, my eyes started looking around for it. Not that long before, he had won the Grammy for best male R & B vocal for a song called "Just Once." I'd been around, but I'd never seen a Grammy up close. I didn't know how to bring it up or how to ask, so I just wandered around, looking to see if it was in a display case or on the mantle over the fireplace. I looked everywhere but it was nowhere to be found.

I finally got the nerve to ask. "Hey, where's your Grammy?"

He said, "Oh, over there."

"Where?"

He pointed toward his daughter's room, "It's over there." It was high up on a bookshelf above her desk.

"Yeah, winning that Grammy was exciting that night," he told me. "But what's more important are my kids. I don't put importance on material things. People would expect me to have all these fancy cars. I've got a Honda minivan to get my kids to school. I've got six kids to get through college."

Make no mistake. He was grateful for winning. But there was a strong lesson on display along with that Grammy in his child's room. No matter what contribution we make to society, or whether we're driving a Ferrari or a Ford, none of it is more important than family. When you have a loving and committed family, you have a remarkable advantage. You go out into the world stronger and with more confidence.

This foundation does require upkeep and maintenance on a daily basis—it's no different than watering your garden or keeping your house clean. Every day, your integrity as a husband, wife, parent, or child will be tested. Things happen that can be upsetting and take you off your mark. Molehills can become mountains very quickly if we don't communicate lovingly and clearly before things get bottled up and resentment builds.

Despite what we might think, our children want us to be firm and strong with them, to be their parent and not their friend. When we don't set and consistently enforce our boundaries, dysfunction follows. If you get upset with your son for borrowing the car without first asking permission and do nothing to punish him, what is that saying about you? What kind of behavior are you modeling for your child?

Why do we so easily put out the welcome mat for all

kinds of harmful behavior, emotional or physical, from members of our family? Many times, these cycles of behavior have been repeated and passed along from one generation to the next. We can make a conscious choice and take action to repair our family relationships. It is within our power to break these cycles here and now. Learning to say "no" and making it clear that you're no longer available for mistreatment takes courage, but it has profound rewards.

I know it's not easy, but many of the ideas we've spoken about that are effective in our relationships in the outside world also work at home, such as teaching people how to treat you. If instead of pointing the finger of blame you learn to express your sadness, disappointment, or anger in a loving way, you have a better chance to make a big inroad. Consider the difference between "How could you do that to me?" and "I need to tell you how I'm feeling about what happened yesterday."

Always remember that work will come and go. Friends will come and go. But your family has a vested interest in you. If we've built a foundation of love in which we cherish, love, and respect one another, we have a refuge. When there are problems, family is there to see us through. Even though our son, Sean, is now a young adult, Karen and I never want him to forget that he can always come home.

THE JOKE'S ON ME

We were on tour in Europe. Traveling with us was a young band, the opening act, and it was their first time out of the

United States. I noticed they were really being careless with their passports and valuables, leaving things out in their unlocked dressing room or unattended on the counter of the hotel lobby. So I reckoned it was time to teach them a lesson.

Seeing the band's passports out yet again, I decided enough was enough. I put them into my pocket and held on to them just long enough to make the kids squirm. Let them think that they'd be stuck in London while we were off to Paris. That would surely make them be more careful. I did it, and they freaked. And I got a good laugh out of it. Immediately after the fact, however, I had second thoughts about the whole thing. I didn't know any of the band members' health histories, and I was taking a risk by creating the kind of stress that could have given somebody a heart attack.

Is it really worth the risk of having humor at someone else's expense? Think about the risk of making gay jokes to someone who is conflicted about their sexuality. Do you have any idea what impact a demeaning and degrading racist or sexist comment might have on someone around you? Add to that list any other off-color jokes about disability or disease. Someone within earshot might hear you and get offended. And lastly, what does making those kinds of jokes say about your character?

When it's used more appropriately, humor is probably the best and easiest way to diffuse tension and lower the stress level in a room. But you have to gauge the situation and know the temperament of the people around you. Some people you work with don't want humor when things are tense. So if you know it's not going to be appreciated, your best option is to take a time out, walk away, get some fresh air, and gain some perspective on the stress situation. With those people, keep your head down, do your work, and try to stay out of artillery range.

If you're calling the shots, a great sense of humor can work wonders, whether you're in charge of a band or a project at your job. We're all under stress. But I think we lead through example. If the musicians I've hired see me having a good time, it gives them permission to also enjoy the experience. If I make a mistake, I laugh about it and say, "Guys, I'm sorry, I made a mistake. I only make three a year. This is the first one." Another mea culpa variation: "Guys, there was a mistake made. It *could* have been me, but it was *probably* not. Let's start it from the beginning." So, when I have a laugh at my expense, I let them know it's OK to make a mistake.

Without humor, you'll have a more challenging time as a leader trying to get everybody on the team to see how important the task is before you. The best result is when everyone has a vested interest, when each person on the team feels that his or her contribution moves you closer to the goal and helps you win. It's OK if they know that you're in charge and you're going to make the final decision.

In my experience, you'll get much better results from being lighthearted than from having a bad attitude, such as "I'm the leader and you'll do as I say and not as I do." Humor that is sensitive and respectful can really be used to create a team atmosphere. You can have fun and be serious at the same time.

I have a friend, a world-renowned neurosurgeon named Dr. Keith Black, of Cedars-Sinai Hospital in Los Angeles. He is someone to whom other doctors send their most difficult cases. Early one afternoon, I was sitting in a conference room to plan a fundraiser for his research institute with some of the most high-powered women in Hollywood. As we waited for Keith to arrive, the conversation veered from donations and invitation lists to curiosity about my work on *American Idol* . . . just as he walked in. The women seemed fascinated about the show and were asking all sorts of questions. "How do you learn so many songs? How do you rehearse? What happens if someone doesn't sing well that day?"

Only minutes before, Keith had his gloved hands inside somebody's skull. The first words out of his mouth would have been just another beaten-to-death cliché coming from another person. And the pause when we quickly looked at one another for agreement before starting to laugh was just as funny as his comment: "Ladies, what Rickey does is amazing, but it's not brain surgery."

I think what I'm doing is important, but in contrast to Dr. Black, I'm not saving any lives. In my opinion, unless you're standing over an operating table with someone's fate in your hands, there's plenty of time to laugh and enjoy your work.

THE TRINITY

Just because you've made it doesn't give you license to rest on your laurels and get lazy. There's always someone behind you who wants your job. If anything, you have to get even more serious about your training to maintain your balance and have any shot at longevity.

I marvel at some of the artists I know like Usher, Mary J. Blige, Beyoncé, and Christina Aguilera. When they walk on stage, they have an amazing power to engage and transform everyone in their presence. The same applies to many of our sports heroes, as well as those we recognize as masters from other fields. How can they make things we know to be so complex appear almost effortless? What is that transcendent quality? That "it" factor?

As we have already explored, it is no accident that they are where they are. As entertainers, they have all the prerequisites: the talent, the voice, the look, and the charisma. They hardly need to be reminded about the importance of preparation. In fact, every time they step out on the stage, they take nothing for granted. They look for every opportunity to raise the bar.

They want perfection, or pretty close to it, in every detail. The music video that lasts only two minutes and the concert performance you see onstage required hundreds if not thousands of hours of preparation. It's no exaggeration that the hairdresser and makeup artist know every note of Beyoncé's songs, because they hear her constantly practicing in their presence.

But another level of preparation that we haven't talked about is at the very essence of the creative spirit. Some people call it "being in the zone." To me it is the regimen of making yourself available to your creativity. You have to put yourself into a state where you can fully allow your creativity to flow.

Here's what you have to do. It's called the Trinity. The Mind, Body, and Spirit. Think of it as your training and exercise program for keeping your creativity in shape. Once you have the Trinity aligned, it's like a domino effect. You will be astonished at the difference it makes. Everything starts to happen because you've opened up the floodgates and unleashed the flow of your good energy.

Here's why this is so important. This thing called life happens. If you are consumed with the problems and worries of the day, it can overload the circuits of your mind. Clearly, that leaves very little room for your mind to create. Likewise, if your spirit is harboring anger, jealousy, hate, or depression, you won't have a great creative range either. Regarding the Body, one might ask, "Why would you have to be in good physical shape to write or perform music?" Being in a creative place is a physically daunting task. When the mind is working that hard, the body feels it. Obviously, any pain, discomfort, or illness in your body will make creative work much more challenging.

Let me emphasize that your creativity is always there, already part of your built-in equipment. It's just that you haven't made yourself available to it. As in any relationship, if you're not open and accessible to your spouse or your friend, you can expect things to go south unless you shift your attitudes and actions into a more positive direction. In the same way, your creativity goes down when you're not tending to it. Like a muscle, it shrinks. It starts out big and shrinks the less you use it. Use it or lose it.

If you're truly serious and committed, you must put the Trinity on your daily schedule. You've got twenty-four hours. In the morning, spend a half hour on your spirit, praying, meditating, gathering your thoughts, or whatever you need to do to calm yourself down so you're relaxed and prepared for the rest of the day. Now that that's done, it's on to the body. You say, "OK, I'm going to spend an hour doing something physical." Again, you have many options: working in the garden, going for a walk, using the treadmill at the gym, or swimming for fifteen minutes and then lifting weights. Make sure it's dedicated focus time, uninterrupted. Then see to it that you have a nutritious and balanced meal. With all that done, this is where your mind comes in. You sit down and you write out a plan for today's activities—not next month's or ten years from now, but today's. If it works better for you, you can even prepare an agenda the night before.

At the end of the day, you can look at the things you've accomplished and the things that still remain on your list. Make yourself a daily checklist.

If taking care of your mind, body, and spirit takes two hours out of your day, then that leaves you with six hours for concentrated work. Since you will be more creative because you're taking care of the Trinity, you may find that you can get a lot more accomplished than others who work ten- or twelve-hour days—six hours will be enough. You have to know when to stop. Go on for too long and your creativity will reach a limit after which there will be diminishing returns.

When you're done for the day, look again at your list and lay out how tomorrow looks. You'll benefit from a good night's sleep.

To make this program work, you will need to prioritize, and you may have to make some tough choices. There won't be as much time to hang out with your friends. They will have to understand that you're hunkered down.

The good news is that you'll see results very quickly. It's self-motivating. Once I'm in the zone, I'm having so much fun that it's hard to stop. Here's one other benefit you'll find: When you are working on something that stimulates your creativity and your passion, you won't mind doing the more tedious parts of your job. For example, it may be outwardly more fun playing music than working on budgets, but I don't mind the budgets in the least. They are part of the pride of ownership.

It's the same when you love your home and value it—you don't mind doing the cleaning chores and housework to keep it up.

You'll find that everything around you starts to radiate with more vitality. You'll notice things that aren't supportive and make changes, especially in your home and work environment. You'll remove the clutter. You'll suddenly paint the walls a warmer, fresher color and add some greenery. Your shortened list of friends will come over and say, "What's with all these plants?" Your answer to them is simple. "Oxygen."

A GOOD BAD DAY

"That's it for me for today. Let's wrap. See you tomorrow."

Every day is not sunshine, especially this one. Everything was off-kilter. The playing was sour. The arrangements seemed like they were all missing the mark. The band knew it. I knew it. I was done. There was nothing left in the tank. There were probably more than a few explanations for why this day had gone from bad to worse. It was a pressure-cooker time leading up to a big show. One artist suddenly dropped out. A new artist wanted a different song that we had to rush to prepare. With that done, there was a last-minute demand that forced us to switch gears again. No matter the reasons, bad days will come up. It's not fun. Musicians' salaries and studio time are not cheap. The deadline was looming.

If you asked people what I was like when I was a young man, they would all say that I was very intense. If we didn't make the deadline on time, I took the blame that I wasn't able to deliver what I said I would. I wanted so much to do a great job that I could be abrasive: "This has to be done, and I need it now. If I needed it tomorrow, I would call you tomorrow. If you can't have it here, I'll call someone else. Someone is waiting for me to deliver this in an hour. I need it now. I need it today. Right now." Phew. I'm sure you get the picture.

The big difference now is that I learned how to be more compassionate, not only toward others, but also toward myself. Most important, I just don't beat myself up anymore. If I know I'm doing the best that's humanly possible, then I feel good about things when I go to bed.

On that particular day, when things started to go sour, I chose to call the session off. Should I instead have found a way to force the situation and fight through it? There was no debate in my mind. My mind was made up that it was time to call it a day, but it definitely did not make the problem go away. It's no different than standing before a big mountain. It looks so high. You know it is a complete waste of energy to fret about how high it is, to get upset, and, as a result, make it look even higher with negative thoughts. Too many of us miss out because we'd rather sit and complain. "Why do I have to climb up to get to the other side? Why can't I just sit here?" The answer is simple: "If you don't go, you won't grow."

Instead, you have three choices in such a situation. You can go over the mountain. You can dig a hole under it. Or you can go around it. The fact is, by sunrise, you have to be on the other side of that mountain. You have to figure out what the best thing is going to be for you. How much time will it take to go around it or go over it? How much power will it take to go through it? So you choose the lesser of the three evils and set about doing it.

When I called the session off, I chose the last option—to go around the mountain. I decided not to fight it. I wasn't going to try to climb over it—it would take too long. I wasn't going to dig under it—it would take too much energy. Instead, my gut told me it was best to go forward with a fresh new plan. When you follow your intuition, you're going to make the right choice most of the time.

Since I was in a frustrated state on that particular day, I had to have that talk with myself. The stresses of the day were intense. There was so much going on at once that I knew I had to stop and shut it down for a minute. Do my homework. Clean everything up. Make new assignments. Realize and accept that this day was gone. There was nothing that I could do about it other than go to bed and look forward to a brighter, better day tomorrow.

The same rules apply when I'm working with an artist who's having a bad day and can't focus. I'll take a break and go off into the corner so we can be private. "Are you OK? I don't want to get into your business. I just want to know if you are OK and if there's anything that I can do." If the answer is "no," then I can say, "Let's just start again tomorrow on a brand-new day. We'll lose a day but we'll still make our deadline. Deal with what you have to deal with. Call me if you need me."

This conversation will either clear the air and let us get on with our work, or make the decision clearer to start fresh tomorrow.

THE GIFT THAT KEEPS ON GIVING

Once you're successful, you're in a better financial position to "give back." It's a wonderful feeling to write a check to a charity and know that your money will have a positive impact on a cause you care about. But the three stories I share with you now talk about another kind of giving that isn't about money, but is just as powerful.

You've most likely never heard of Christine Bradley. She's just another one of those behind-the-scenes people who work to make sure everything looks easy and effortless on your television screen at home. She's an associate director, and she's one of the best at what she does. Her job is to line up every shot and map out every detail for the director. Because music programming is her specialty, she even went back to school and took music courses so she'd understand everything that was going on.

We were working with director Marty Callner on an HBO special with Whitney Houston called *Classic Whitney*. I had a lot on my plate. Assemble a forty-two-piece orchestra. Get all the arrangements together. Rehearse the band. Get Whitney ready. On top of all of that, I had to go through each song, moment by moment, with Christine.

"The flute solo happens here. That person's located here on the stage. The background vocals come in right here. This goes on for eight bars."

This went on and on, this dissection of the show, bit by bit. It was intense. I could tell that she was getting stressed out.

"When do the French horns come in? Is that stage right or stage left?"

"Hold it for a minute," I told her.

I got up from the table and went over and popped a CD into the sound system. The deep, unmistakable voice of Barry White filled the room.

She was on autopilot and didn't bother to look up from her papers. "Wait! I can't find this in my notes. What song is this? Are we doing this song?"

"Can't get enough of your love, baby."

"No," I said. "This is called a Barry Break."

"Never going to give you up."

A few seconds later, I turned the CD off and said, "OK, now, let's get back to work." Sometimes it really helps to take a break and do something totally different. You'll have a better perspective afterward, guaranteed.

Some time later, I was rehearsing for a television show called *Genius: A Night for Ray Charles*. The producer was Ken Ehrlich. He's known for his revolutionary vision as executive producer of the Grammys, the Emmys, and many other television music specials. As usual, Ken was walking around the rehearsal wearing his headset like an NFL coach. When we took a short pause between songs, Ken sat there, a little self-conscious, playing the piano.

As he went back into the booth, we were getting set to start in on the next song, "Tell Me What I Say." Al Green came out to sing the vocal.

"You should play," I told Ken through his headset.

"I should play?"

"Yeah. You should play the piano. Look, put your headset down and come on up."

I knew he wanted to play. He had been hovering around, watching and looking. He wanted to participate. Even though it was his show and he was signing the checks, it would be crossing a boundary of professionalism, it would be a breach of etiquette. I can see the smile on his face as if it were yesterday. Needless to say, Ken was a happy man, and so was I.

One morning back in 2003, I got a call from Candace Bond-McKeever, an executive at *Essence* magazine. Luther Vandross was booked to do the *Essence* Music Festival in New Orleans. He had just suffered a massive stroke. It was a few short weeks before the show.

Candace said, "Luther can't perform now. What should we do? Should we book someone else?"

I thought for a second. "Why not do a tribute to Luther?" I suggested to her. "Everyone is coming there expecting to hear these Luther Vandross songs. I think it would be really great to use his entire band and crew. They know all the songs inside and out, and I'm sure they could use the work." I told Candace that I could probably get a number of A-list singers to participate.

When the performance actually took place, there was high emotion as everybody at the Superdome in New Orleans was singing along note by note with the artists. I noticed members of the band crying before, during, and after every song.

Some years ago, I got a call from a Washington Preparatory High School music instructor named Fernando Pullum. Music education was (and still is) on the endangered species list in most public schools.

I offered to give them arrangements from the television shows I was working on and come back one week later to see what they'd done with them. From time to time, we'd get the students all packed into a school bus so they could be included in some of the big music industry events I was doing. At rehearsals, I'd let them come and sit in. I loved seeing these young people holding their instruments, sitting on the bandstand beside the masters of their instruments.

Each of these students got a bird's-eye view of what it takes to make it. The look of wonderment on their faces and the appreciation they felt for this opportunity was something I'll always carry with me. I could see myself as a young kid in each of them. But well beyond that, I could see that they were watching and saying, "I can see *myself* sitting up there. Now I know what he does, I know what it takes. I will do it." Not "I want to do it" or "I don't know if I can do it," but "I will do it."

From that group of kids, I stayed in touch with the young bass player in the group and became a mentor to him. It has been an incredible joy and satisfaction for me to watch him develop. He is now graduating from Berklee School of Music.

Immediately after the Luther tribute, several of the band members approached me and said thank you. "Not only do we need the money, but it's closure for us. This is probably the last time we'll ever be together and play this show. We didn't know the last time we played with Luther that it would be the final one. This gave us a chance to all be together."

Ken Ehrlich came up to me after he did the song with Al Green. He was like a small child who could barely contain his excitement. "Thank you, man. That was cool."

And whenever Christine Bradley sees me at the Grammys or some other program we're working on, she takes off her headset, tilts her head back, and says, "I think it's time for a Barry Break."

In truth, there's nothing so spectacular about the stories I just told you.

The fact of the matter is that I got just as much (and probably more) from giving of myself in these experiences as the recipients did. My main purpose in telling them is to emphasize that when we give to each other with love and selfless intention, there's an amazing payoff. If your intentions are right, your rewards will not be short-lived.

I give you these stories as a warm-up to even more powerful things that you can do. It's not only about writing a check. When you extend this giving spirit to people who are truly in need of a helping hand and/or encouragement, it is even more powerful.

I've also worked with older foster kids who are being emancipated out of the system. These young people are given a few dollars and told, "Good luck—you're eighteen now, and the government can't help you anymore."

Each and every one of us has had to deal with issues of abandonment and neglect to some degree. But few of us can imagine what these kids have to go through. More than half of all foster children end up as prostitutes and homeless. Consider the impact of helping just one of them avoid that fate.

Whatever your talent and passion, you have something valuable to contribute. If you are good at writing or math, tutor a child at the local school. Ask that elderly person in the neighborhood if you can help them with shopping, do their yard work, or walk their dog.

You still might be thinking, "I've got a busy life. I'm a good person, but I just don't have the time. What's in it for me?"

It's called "instant karma." Not next week, not next year.

You do something, then sit back and watch what happens. You'll get the satisfaction of knowing that you've extended far beyond yourself.

To repeat, for emphasis: If your intentions aren't right, your rewards will be short-lived. If you give a little only so that you can gain some specific advantage in return, you will only get a little.

Whatever the circumstance, if you don't take the opportunity to give to others, you're the one losing out. No matter how busy we are, we can always squeeze in something extra that can make a difference.

QUALITY CONTROL

When I'm not making music, chances are I'm listening to it. Whether I'm in my studio or in my car, I'm playing back all the songs we did yesterday and the day before that. It doesn't matter if it's Aretha Franklin or one of the *Idol* contestants. It could be a rough rehearsal tape or a clip from the live broadcast. They all get the same treatment.

I'm listening for good reasons. A small but very important element may be off that I didn't catch in rehearsal. On top of that, there's always room for improvement. I told the horn player to play a note an octave higher to get more power at a certain part of the song. Did he remember to do it? If so, did it really have the payoff I had envisioned? That new arrangement for the strings may still need work. With fresh ears, I can listen for all the details.

Outsiders may think, "He's so successful, he doesn't have

to do that kind of thing anymore. He certainly shouldn't have to review his work." They're wrong. I constantly go over every element, painstakingly. If you have a better idea, please call or e-mail me. It's the only way I know to maintain quality control. I've done the same steps over and over again for my entire career.

So this idea about going the extra mile and giving people more than they expect is not something that's just for beginners.

Sorry. It's a commitment for life. I know what you're thinking. "I don't want to hear this." You probably wish that I had left this little piece of information out of the book. But we've gone this far. The truth is that no matter how successful you become, you'll have to prove yourself on a daily basis. Otherwise, there are plenty of people lining up to take your job.

You've heard about elite athletes who get more serious about their training regimen as they get older, continuously analyzing hour after hour of video of both their performance and the competition's. It's no different in my world.

OK, but there is some good news with all of this. With your success behind you, you have a huge advantage over that younger, less experienced version of yourself. I'm not just talking about the obvious—the wisdom and know-how that come with age and experience. Instead, the great thing is that you don't have to do it alone. Because you're accomplished now, you not only get to choose your team, but the best players will want to come and be on your side. Everyone wants to be on a winning team.

Here's just one example. I cannot even think about how much more difficult my job would be without Ernie Fields, Jr. He is Kool Man Kool. He's my contractor, meaning that he hires all the musicians and staff for any job I do. He works out all the contracts, calculates the budgets, works out the union requirements, and so on—you name it. He's been with me for years. At age seventy-four he still practices his woodwinds and plays with the band. He's also like a father to me, who I turn to on matters both business and personal when I get stuck. He not only takes care of business. His spirit lets you know he's someone who's there for reasons more important than getting a paycheck.

On the other end of the spectrum, I enjoy hiring young kids. I look for that intangible spark of promise in them. Sometimes it takes them a little bit of time to get it. But often, you get someone right off the bat who is willing to roll up his or her sleeves and get the work done. You have the best of both worlds when your team members are happy with the job they're doing and feel an equal benefit that they're growing and being enriched through the experience. Sprinters talk about the importance of relaxation as they kneel in the starting blocks with every muscle ready to explode. A relaxed mind performs better.

HE'S GOT IT MADE

People nod at you when you walk by, their eyes saying, "Man, he's got it made." Everybody thinks that you live like some kind of god in a heavenly realm, the wheels of your luxury car floating a few inches above the pavement. With your privilege and checkbook, the problems of everyday life that the rest of us deal with can be swatted away like an annoying gnat. Right?

Don't expect the velvet ropes to open and move you out of harm's way from personal avalanches, earthquakes, and other life forces out of our control. While we're at it, don't assume you'll be immune from financial worries either. When you have a lot of money, there's a lot more to lose. You have to make sound decisions.

Think about it for a moment. You've done as I've recommended and worked hard. You've walked into each situation as fully prepared and focused as possible. People like working with you, and you make things happen. You're there now, finally. Then how can it be that you feel so empty—perhaps even miserable? You may question whether the whole thing was worth it after all. "Is *this* all there is?" Feeling vulnerable, your ego may come visiting again, whispering in your ear, "I'm so successful. I shouldn't feel this way."

Success breeds its own special set of challenges. Because you've been good at setting the bar high, the people around you have an equally high expectation of you. You're constantly delivering and being there for others. When you're a so-called important person, people may be less forgiving if you're having an off day or are in a funk emotionally, spiritually, or physically. The scrutiny is there. You can't even scratch your head without them thinking that there's something wrong. If you have a medical problem or if you're getting older and moving a little slower in your mind or body, rumors will start flying. The telephone game will have you all but dead and buried.

The more successful you become, the more careful you have to be about how you spend your time. Time is money. Please don't take this the wrong way. We all want to be good listeners. It's a wonderful character trait. But let's face it. We all have people around us who will talk our ears off and try to push every button to get us off-task and caught up in their personal stuff. It may behoove you to learn the art of selective listening. It means tuning out what isn't important, like not clogging the hard drive of your mind with endless bits and fragments that will slow it down and distract it from the important tasks at hand.

This is particularly useful if you're stressed out. Some people get angry and mean and start yelling and screaming when they've reached their threshold. I go the opposite way and pull back. I only talk when I need to talk. And again, I only listen when I need to listen. I have to make a judgment call about whether the information I'm hearing is useful and fits into the situation right then and there.

When you're successful, the people who work for you will look to you for leadership. They put you under the microscope when a challenging situation comes up. "Hmm, how is he going to handle this situation?"

At the same time, they also want to know that you're fallible. If I'm going through a stressful time, there's one way the people around me can show their support. It's by doing what they're supposed to do. That way, I will have one less thing to worry about.

If I show signs of being a little more reserved and quiet than usual, the band and staff understand that it's my way of handling stress. My guys know if I'm silent, pensive, and reflective, it means I'm going through some stuff. Therefore, they don't have to come up to me and say, "Rickey, what's wrong?" They can feel the energy, too, that the circuits are overloaded. It's my way of slowing things down to break it down and deal with one situation at a time. I'm human, too.

This is a very difficult art to practice—to be both engaged and detached at the same time. It has to be a perfect balancing act. If you veer off to one side, you'll be perceived as shallow and phony. Go the other direction, and you're cold, unfeeling, self-absorbed, or stuck-up.

Here's what's helpful to me to always remember. Everybody in your life needs a touch, a little physical, human touch. If they don't get it, they feel neglected. Think about it, seriously. Everybody needs an opportunity to be *number one*, even for just a few moments. No one takes kindly to being number two forever. What's the most common complaint in divorce cases involving a famous person? "He (or she) was too busy and never had time for me."

One other very important thing to reemphasize: Don't forget to put yourself on that list. If you're not taking care of yourself, sit back and watch the wheels fall off. It's like running your car without oil. So again, please make sure you give yourself that special touch as well. Remember the section on the Trinity? It's why I love to go and pull weeds in my backyard, even though I could have the gardener do it. It's what works for me. That's the special touch I reserve for me.

DON'T FORGET YOUR PASS

One by-product of having a busy life is that I'm on a first-name basis with almost every security guard at the studios in Hollywood. I'm constantly in and out, running from the studio to meetings and errands.

There was a big movie star back in the 1930s and '40s

named George Raft. He was famous for playing gangsters and tough guys, but when that movie genre faded from popularity, so did he. His descent was also aided by a bad streak of misjudgment, the Midas touch in reverse. Raft became a legend for turning down roles in a host of movies that went on to become classics. In one film, the fact that his character had to die at the end was the reason he allegedly nixed it. The part went instead to an up-and-coming actor: *High Sierra* proved to be the big breakthrough for Humphrey Bogart. If that wasn't bad enough, Raft also reportedly turned down the lead in *Casablanca*. The reason? He didn't want to play opposite the then-unknown Ingrid Bergman.

"The people you meet on the way up are the same ones you meet on the way down." Raft's sage words of advice had a certain gravitas, because he knew what he was talking about. No matter how big and successful you may think you are—and how much bigger your salary is than the others—there is never any excuse for being anything less than polite and respectful to others.

If you believe in ghosts, then the spirit of George Raft was surely hanging around the studio one day and letting me know how annoyed he was with me. I was the music director for a big awards program. It was show day, and as usual, I was rushing in and out of the venue all day long. Again, most of the security guards know me.

The show was about to start, live on the air in twelve minutes. I had a few minutes to take care of a problem. My guests were outside, and they had phoned me to say that they were having trouble getting in to see the show. "Not again," I fumed. They were on the list, or so I thought. We had even double-checked.

I walked out past the front gate. My friends were standing there, and a few seconds later everything was fixed. Now there were five minutes remaining before air.

I headed back toward the gate. I looked up and there was this new security guard who I had never seen before. The guy said to me, "Where's your pass?" I put my hand on my chest and realized suddenly that I had left it on the table of my dressing room when I changed into my show wardrobe.

I said, "Sorry, man, I should have my pass. I don't have it. I'm the music director. The show's going to start in five minutes. I've got to get back in. My guys are waiting for me to go on stage."

The guard said to me, "I don't care who you think you are. You are not going through this gate without proper credentials."

"You call the head of security right now," I huffed and I puffed. "I'm going in and you tell him that I'm going in."

That was not the end of the story. The security guard got so angry with me that it degenerated into a shouting match. Very smart. . . . There was little me, teeth gnashing and growling in the grille of a guy who was six-foot-two, two hundred and fifty pounds. Regardless, he called Marvel, the head of security, who, coincidentally, happened to have been a good friend of my uncle Frank. In fact, they had been partners years ago in a security business.

"Let Rickey do whatever he wants to do."

I bolted through with thirty seconds left to showtime.

I couldn't wait until the end of the show. I didn't want to leave things like they were for any longer than necessary. At the first commercial break, I ran out to the guy to apologize.

I told him, "It's not personal. I'm not angry with you. I don't want you to be angry with me. I realize you're just doing your job. I should have had my pass. I didn't want to show any disrespect to you. I'm sorry."

Well, by the end of the short conversation, he had invited me to have dinner with him and his wife after the show.

The moral of the story is that you can turn it around. You can laugh about it. Every time I see him now at a show, we have a running joke. He says to me, "Where's your pass?"

We could have kept things where they had been at five minutes to airtime. I could have held on to the hostility toward him that would just gnaw away at me every time I saw him. He, in turn, would no doubt have had only bad things to say about me. "This guy thinks that he runs the world and he doesn't need a pass." That, of course, was not the case. I had just forgotten it.

People understand that we all make mistakes. I just blew up at him. I was wrong—and the first step was to admit it to myself and to the guard. "I'll be more careful the next time." I couldn't say to him, "It won't happen again," because nobody can guarantee that. You've got to keep it real. "I'll watch it in the future."

People are constantly creating those little toxic pockets around themselves. Sometimes these situations are unavoidable. People's feelings get hurt. They may feel slighted, disrespected, and you may never know about it until years later.

Negativity is a complete waste of time, going nowhere fast and lower than ground zero. Regardless of your differences, you'll walk into any situation with a gaping chip on your shoulder if you don't have a fundamental respect for other human beings.

You've heard it before, but I'll say it again. Everyone has their own form of personal power. If somebody can make you angry, then you've given that power away. It's like saying to that person, "Hey, why don't you just take control of me and tell me how I should feel?"

"He was short with me." "He didn't look at me." "She didn't say what I wanted her to say." Listen to the hissing sound as the air leaks out of your balloon.

How many days do I drive in past the guard gate worried about whether someone has taken my reserved parking spot? Or if my fettuccine is going to be there in my dressing room as I had requested? Or if my socks really match my trousers? Think about all the energy and time wasted on worry and negativity. On this point, I recently got a simple but powerful reminder. A homeless lady downtown asked me for some spare change. It turned into a fifteen-minute conversation. I learned she was from the San Francisco area. She said, "It's gotten cold up there." She had recently come back down to L.A. and was a little down on her luck.

"What a beautiful day it is today. The temperature is just right. I don't have to put on a coat or take one off. This sweat-shirt is all I need," she said.

I could tell that this was not some lip service to shake a little more sympathy and money from me. Her eyes told me that it was true that things were bad, but equally true to her, it was still a beautiful day.

The homeless woman taught me that the decision is solely in your hands to make it a beautiful day or not. Why do so many of us make the choice to remain in a negative, anxiety-ridden, fearful state of mind, whether we're sitting on a piece of cardboard on the sidewalk, on a comfortable sofa in front of the TV, or on a posh leather car seat hurrying past the guard gate?

Hey, where's your pass?

Jump on the Next Train

The energy intensifies as the competition heats up toward the finale. On Tuesdays and Wednesdays when we go live, the studio feels like it's in the middle of a hurricane. Whether their instrument is a guitar, a steam iron, a makeup brush, a teleprompter keyboard, or a camera crane, everyone is tuned and ready to perform on cue.

It would be natural for any of us to say that this is just another gig, but it's clearly not. Whether we're on camera, off to the side of the stage, backstage, or in the booth, we all know that every little move is under the microscope. Millions of people treat what we are doing as part of a weekly ritual, families and friends get together to watch and talk about every little nuance, picking apart what they liked and didn't like, feeding on the drama that one of their favorites will disappear in this version of musical chairs.

Beyond all the games, egos, and intrigues, the contestants are no different from the rest of us who are striving to succeed in our lives. In order to succeed, we all have to begin by finding that place inside of us where there is quiet, focus, and peace. There is certainty in the fact that if you're fearful, your odds of winning Idol or anything else are greatly diminished. If that kind of negative energy runs unchecked on a daily basis, it is going to eat you alive.

So you have to find a way to put it aside. You have to understand that it is not an accident that out of 100,000 people, you were chosen to compete and then made it to the top 12. And now, suddenly, you're in the finals.

For those who dream about being on American Idol, becoming a film star, or playing in professional sports, the odds are daunting. As I've said before, even if you have the talent, there are thousands of people who want the same job. It is a sad fact that not everybody who competes is able to win. There's not enough room. To love it is not enough. Go ahead and pursue your dream, but remember that you must make a living. You must provide for yourself. Along the way, it is a fact of life that you will have to compromise and do jobs that you don't want to do. Ask almost anybody who's "made it," and you'll hear them use the the word "tenacity" over and over again to describe the quality that kept them alive and in the hunt.

What I say to each contestant on American Idol is that it's about recognizing who you are, where you are, and what you want out of it. You have to accept that this way of life is not for everybody. There's a price to be paid for success. I've already told you how just the hours I have to work are enough to poison the dreams that some may have of being like me.

Put yourself in the shoes of one of those final contestants. You've seen from the others' misfortune how easy it is to implode. Now you're standing alone in the hallway by the restrooms. You're minutes away from taking the stage. No one would dare to come up and bother you, unless your wardrobe or makeup needed a last-second touch-up. You now know exactly how that gladiator or samurai in one of those epic movies felt as he stood alone before the pivotal battle, summoning up *every ounce of courage and making his concentration as sharp as his sword.*

How do we really get to that true place of fearlessness? The next important breakthrough is to realize that all of this is temporary, including your existence. When you accept that fact, you become in tune with your journey and realize that the Idol process is pretty close to real life. Like your life, it is impermanent and goes by so fast. Like your life, you must get everything out of it that you can. Like your life, everything you do is not going to turn into gold.

So every time you sing, it will not be the perfect vocal, because there is no such thing as a perfect vocal. There is no perfect life. You go through ups and downs. You go through performances when you do really well, and others where you do poorly. It all boils down to the preparation. It is about how you take each challenge that presents itself. It's about getting the most out of every day.

When you have that attitude, you can leave the fear behind. You're able to be fully present and appreciate each breath and each heartbeat. In that state of mind, we can better give and receive the love that surrounds us in so many forms.

My biggest challenge has been that I can't seem to turn the music off in my head. During my sleep, there's always a little music happening. There are chords, vocals, and tunes that won't go out of my mind. My breakthrough on that was to finally understand something. It's a simple answer: My life is music. There is no separation.

So back to our story. You have already gotten the sense that there's a lot that happens in the life of the Idol contestant in the course of three months. That journey for the young person pacing the hallway about to sing in the final can indeed almost feel like a lifetime. Let me walk you through the process a bit more closely, so you'll get a fuller sense of what it feels like on the inside.

Let's go back to the beginning, when the contestants meet me for the first time. They have already sat down with executive producers Nigel Lythgoe and Ken Warwick. The Dream Team—Michael Orland, Matt Rohde, Debra Byrd, and Dorian Holley—work closely with the contestants to help them sort through their choices, rehearse, and determine the best way to perform their final song choice. Each performance can be no longer than a minute and fifteen seconds or a minute and a half, tops, depending on the length of the show that particular night. Then they're ready to meet with me.

By this time, I've already listened to a tape of their rehearsal. I've gone through it and made my notes. The key may be too high or too low. Or they may need to make tempo adjustments. I might say to them, "I've listened to you sing. When you get to this part, I'm going to hold the note longer to give you time. Do you think you can do that?" It's usually at a pivotal place that can make them sound more dynamic, bigger, and stronger. On the other hand, if there's a note they can't hit, I can move quickly off it. If they crack at that note, I may give them alternate notes to sing. In fact, the judges might hear it and say, "Wow, that was original. They're putting their own personality into it!"

I might suggest that they sing with just an acoustic guitar or a piano instead of the full band. Or maybe that they just do the first line a cappella. All of these techniques are ways to make it creative for them and give them a chance to show their personality.

They sometimes listen to their vocal and say, "This doesn't

sound good." *Most of the time, they're right. They then have to go and make their own adjustments and practice. When they come to see me the next day—it's show day—we run it one more time. As I said, when they think it sounds bad, it's usually not their insecurities speaking. Good is good, and bad is bad. But there are still people who are in denial. I say to them, "You should listen to it again, and listen for this particular part. You need to make some adjustments about how you're hitting the note because it's coming out too flat." I'll tell them, "I've heard you sing it correctly." As you've already heard, sometimes they take the advice, and sometimes they don't.*

But at the end of the day, everybody you see on the show is there for a good reason. Sometimes, truth be told, it's not necessarily because of their ability to sing in tune. Some very successful people can't. Anyone watching the show can see that some contestants go from zero to sixty in just a few weeks. If you're a good singer and you've suddenly got a large orchestra behind you, that's great support.

You have to start with raw talent that can be shaped. If you don't have that, it doesn't matter how many coaches and award-winning people you have around you.

There's no artist who is "the perfect package." And if they were the perfect package, we'd have to add the words "for now." Beauty, style, grace, and looks will fade with time. You can't bank on those things for longevity in your career. Another important point: Not everybody is supposed to have longevity. People are always coming and going.

Whether you are fortunate enough to be a one-hit wonder or have many hits, you have to understand, recognize, and accept when a particular part of your journey has run its course. As an athlete you have to make adjustments if your pitching arm can't throw a baseball 100 miles an hour any longer. Aretha may not be able to hit the same range that she could when she was eighteen, but she still makes you feel every note she sings. You need to constantly make adjustments.

Remember that even the best game plan does not guarantee success. Olympic gold medals, Super Bowl rings, and other championships are often decided by fractions of seconds or millimeters. Your game plan brought you to the starting blocks and may have helped you prepare for this opportunity, but in the heat of the battle, your adjustments will be the determining factor. Your biggest adjustment may be knowing to stop when something has run its course. A better way to look at it is to recognize when it's time to get off one train and jump on to a new one. I stress that because a successful life is a series of connected dots. All too often it happens—if you stay too long you may miss the connection by a week, a year, several years, or even a decade because you thought you were going to be able to ride this one for the rest of your life. If that doesn't happen, it doesn't mean that you lost your talent. It's not the kiss of death. It's that the public isn't buying what you're selling.

So the final breakthrough for Idol *contestants is to recognize that they are gifted human beings beyond their talent in singing. They have more gifts than one. And they should explore those other gifts. All this passion they brought with them to* American Idol *to be a singer? Well, guess what? Those same qualities—the tenacity, dedication, persistence, passion, and focus—will take them through many other wonderful and exciting doors. You could become a manager, a record company owner, a publisher, a writer, an arranger, a musician, or a discoverer of new talent.*

For those young people on the show, Idol *is a thrill ride equal to a million roller coasters. And then after three months, the brakes are applied—heavily. Boom! Only one person wins, and those not fortunate to get a record deal or other major opportunity from all the exposure often go back to zero, sometimes in a day. One day, everybody knows your name and talks about you at the water cooler at work. The next day, no one even remembers that you were on the show.*

When it's time to say good-bye, I give the contestants some parting words as they have no other choice but to move on to their next train. I tell them that I hope they'll feel only gratitude for the invaluable experience and perspective that the Idol *process has given them. As we have seen, not everyone who is left standing at the end has a guaranteed ticket to a stellar singing career. There are lots of other directions to go in, as past* Idol *alumni have demonstrated. Choices abound: theater, movies, and commercials, as well as pursuing their music careers. It's a matter of spotting the next train coming and jumping on it.*

THE ROAD AHEAD

Each and every one of the stories in this book illustrates how a certain behavior, attitude, or outlook has the power to propel us forward on the highway, slow us down, or in the worst case, lead us to the nearest exit.

If you have made it to the end of this book, I hope that you have found something above and beyond the anecdotes and commentaries to hold your attention. As a musician, I know about pitch, rhythm, harmony, and resonance. Music has a frequency, an immediate and heartfelt connection that either draws us in or repels us, just like the words on these pages. This is why one particular song—out of the millions of love songs that have ever been written—will sometimes speak to us like no other.

My song to you comes back to the same refrain. "If a guy like Rickey Minor can do it, so can I." I hope you've noticed something else that is implicit between the lines: You don't need to take a sledgehammer to your life to make it better. All you really need is a chisel.

Why only a chisel? Remember the contestant on *Idol* who thought he needed a lot of razzle-dazzle to make an impression? The night before the show, his sledgehammer struck a mighty blow on the song he had been preparing all week. Is that really what the judges are looking for and what makes the viewers choose one person over another? I guess not.

Ryan Seacrest tapped him on the shoulder the very next day to send him home.

What qualities of performance make the critical difference? Usually, they are almost imperceptible: the intensity in that beat of silence just before the song's final phrase; the poignant gaze from the singer's eyes that convinced you of her honesty; or that invincible confidence that showed she was prepared, masterful, and "looked like a winner." In the end, perhaps it was the simplicity, authenticity, and integrity of *not trying* to be anything other than who she truly was.

Not unlike the reaction to a song from the judges and viewers of *Idol*, you will get immediate feedback to the subtlest of changes you make with your chisel. In the same way that I got that math problem horribly wrong on my test by committing a slight mistake, making a positive change to fix it, even of the smallest nature, set off a chain reaction. Don't be surprised. Suddenly, your family, friends, or co-workers may feel the shift in your energy, noticeably more positive and less toxic.

Slowly but surely, goals in your life that were once the source of anxiety and fear will no longer wreak havoc on your emotions and overall health and well-being. Situations that used to continually result in rejection become successes with half the effort. You begin to feel a sense of accomplishment. The contribution of your talents is appreciated. You find greater joy in being part of a team. Without even having to think about it, you have become even more confident, emboldened, and committed to the process of your inner growth. The idea of giving people more than what they were expecting is no longer a lofty aspiration. It is embodied seamlessly in your work, a natural consequence of your actions.

From reading this book, you have already begun a transformation that may be hard for you to notice. Some issues in your own life that had been hidden from view may begin to surface. Maybe you've recognized how one or two of those factors was having a detrimental influence on your life.

For some of you, this book may bring to the surface more challenging feelings. If you have any disturbing emotions that come up as a consequence, know that this is a normal part of the process when you've held something inside for so long. If you get stuck or feel debilitating pain or depression, remember that you don't have to go through it alone. There are professionals who can help you work through it. There's usually a major breakthrough waiting for you on the other side.

As you move forward, remember that your chisel must always be at hand, ready to make the small adjustments and corrections you will need to keep growing and flourishing. There's a simple explanation for this: With every breath, your entire being goes through changes. Nothing is static. We are continuously in transformation. We are different today from the way we were yesterday, or will be tomorrow or even ten minutes from now.

There would be nothing more gratifying for me than if, today, tomorrow, or sometime in the future, something you've read on these pages motivates you to take a step forward in at least one aspect of your life. The choice is yours. When things start to come together, you'll be encouraged and excited about each new step you're about to take. You'll begin to see for yourself that no matter what life serves up—good or bad, triumphs or setbacks—the road ahead will always be clear.

Acknowledgments

First and foremost, I give thanks to God Almighty through whom all blessings flow. To my wife, Karen, you have been steadfast in your convictions for our marriage and our family, never wavering, the one person that I can always count on to be honest and truthful. You are my partner, my lover, and my best friend. I love you. To my son, Sean, I'm so proud of all that you've accomplished and equally moved by the man that you've become. The future lies in your capable hands.

My heartfelt thanks goes out to David Brokaw, who encouraged me to write this book and put the wheels in motion. Joel Brokaw, the time spent with you was both enjoyable and enlightening. Thank you for helping me find my voice and organize my thoughts. Thank you to my literary agent, Paul Bresnick, for his drive and determination to get my book published, and to William Shinker, publisher of Gotham books, for his belief in my story. Thanks to my editors, Jessica Sindler and Erin Moore; art designer, Ray Lundgren; publicist, Jaime McDonald; photographer, Rob Shanahan; and the entire staff at Gotham Books.

Thanks to my mom, Helen Blevins, for her encouragement and belief that I could become anything that I desired. To Uncle Frank, for putting me on the right path, and Aunt Dixie, for helping me find some of the old family photos. To my siblings, Kathy Minor, Victor Minor, Cheryl Blevins, and John Blevins, Jr., may God continue to bless you and your families.

To Mildred and George McMillan. You've blessed me with

your daughter and kept me in your heart and prayers. Thanks for all the wonderful memories, especially the holiday gatherings. Also, thanks to my brothers-in-law, Kenneth, Keith, and Kirk McMillan. Your kindness shall never be forgotten.

To my musical family and staff. I can always count on you guys to be there for me: Ernie Fields, Jr., Teddy Campbell, Paul Jackson, Jr., Dave Delhomme, Kevin Ricard, Herman Jackson, Wayne Linsey, Sharlotte Gibson, Sy Smith, Kenya Hathaway, Dorian Holley, Harry Kim, Diane Louie, Debbie Chase, Rob Leifer, Robert Boyd, and Wayne Holmes.

To all of the musicians, singers, artist, arrangers, copyists, managers, record executives, producers, directors, agents, production assistants, people in craft services, and security guards. All too many names to mention, I thank you from the bottom of my heart. You are a vital part of the fabric that makes me and holds me together. And finally to my grandmother Donia Minor, who undoubtedly changed the course of my life with just one decision, to seek a better life. Your gentle spirit lives in my soul.

As I sit and reflect on my journey to this point in my life, I'm humbled by God's grace and mercy. Why me? I believe it's because God decides and appoints us individually.

> *"To whom much is given, much is required"*
> —Luke 12:48

Which simply means that I've been entrusted to share with you the readers the infinite possibilities we all share. First, we must forgive ourselves for our imperfections and make a commitment to leave a positive mark in this world and love without prejudice. We need one another more now than ever. Start today and move toward the light of your soul and free your mind from the bondage of your past.

ABOUT THE AUTHOR

Rickey Minor is the Emmy-nominated music director of *American Idol* and the Grammy Awards. He has served as music director for almost every major American awards show, including the Super Bowl. He has worked with Whitney Houston, Christina Aguilera, Alicia Keys, Usher, Ray Charles, The Dixie Chicks, Mary J. Blige, Beyoncé Knowles, Stevie Wonder, Herbie Hancock, Sting, Aretha Franklin, and many others. He lives in Los Angeles with his wife, Karen.

650.1 M

Minor, Rickey.
There's no traffic on the extra
mile